Ultimate
STOCK CAR

Ultimate
STOCK CAR

BILL CENTER

DORLING KINDERSLEY

Dorling **DK** Kindersley

LONDON, NEW YORK, SYDNEY, DELHI, PARIS,
MUNICH, and JOHANNESBURG

Senior Editor Jill Hamilton
Publisher Sean Moore
Editorial Director LaVonne Carlson
Art Director Tina Vaughan

Designed and developed by
TEHABI BOOKS
Editorial Director Nancy Cash
Editor Terry Spohn
Design Director Andy Lewis
Art Director Curt Boyer

First American Edition, 2000

2 4 6 8 10 9 7 5 3 1

Published in the United States by
Dorling Kindersley Publishing Inc.
95 Madison Avenue
New York, NY 10016

Library of Congress Cataloging-in-Publication Data

Center, Bill.
    Ultimate stock car / Bill Center
        p. cm.
    Includes index.
    ISBN 0-7894-5967-1
    1. Stock cars (Automobiles). 2. Stock car racing. I. Title.

TL236.28 .C46 2000
796.72'0973--dc21   00-035898

This edition is printed on acid-free paper that meets the American
National Standards Institute Z39.48 Standard.

Printed by Dai Nippon Printing Co., Ltd., Hong Kong

Contents

PART THREE

RACING PERSONALITIES
154–183

Author's preface

THE STRENGTH AND BEAUTY of stock car racing is found in what should be the fatal flaw – the car. The mass-produced American passenger car was never intended to be a racing vehicle. Although Henry Ford launched his empire with money won in one of America's first automobile races, his goal was to create transportation for the masses. Cars that rolled off Detroit's assembly lines focused on style and practicality more than speed and power. The traditional American race car was developed as an open-wheel hybrid at the cutting edge of technology. Passenger cars were at the other end of the spectrum. That changed as soon as friends began comparing Chevys to Fords and Oldsmobiles to Dodges. The cornerstone of stock car racing is the brag, "My car is faster than yours." Stock car racing took root, not in factories, but in garages across the land with men – some with shady reasons, such as running moonshine – who rightfully believed they could improve on Detroit. They went from drag racing to dirt ovals to superspeedways. And they took America along for the ride. Cars have become an extension of people and families. Some swear by Fords. Others would never drive one. They prefer Chevys or Buicks or Chryslers. And there lies the secret formula that NASCAR founder Bill France uncovered more than half a century ago. Put talented drivers in the family sedan and let them race. Who would pay to see that? Millions.

BILL CENTER

▼ **FAST FORD**
This 1956 Ford won Ford's first Southern 500 victory at Darlington, South Carolina, with an average speed of 95.167 mph, the fastest in NASCAR history at the time.

Foreword

When I began car racing back in 1946, it was just something to do. We just did it because we loved to race. They called those little old cars we drove "modifieds," but we really didn't know a whole lot about modifying them. Both the cars and engines were pretty much stock back then. I guess you can say we grew along with the sport. We kept trying new things to make the cars run faster than the next guy. The biggest step in turning them from stock cars into true race cars came when NASCAR said we could do anything underneath the car as long as it was good workmanship. I guess you can say they just turned us loose. Aerodynamics are a big thing now, but not really a new thing. Like everything else in stock car racing, it has just gotten bigger and better. I remember back in 1970 when Buddy Baker was driving for me at Daytona. We were getting outrun pretty good, so I moved the fenders out about four inches and immediately picked up three mph. It's amazing how far we have come since then, but then again, maybe it isn't. We're all racers. Our job is to outrun the other guy and we'll try whatever we can to do it. The difference is how big a business it has become. You can take ten of us who ran back in the 1950s and '60s, put all the winnings together, and Dale Jarrett won more than that in the 2000 Daytona 500. What started out as just something to do – a love to go fast – has turned into the fastest-growing sport in the country.

Cotton Owens

COTTON OWENS

THE HISTORY OF STOCK CAR RACING

1

The mystique of stock car racing crosses eras of machinery and racetracks as well as men. The Ford Taurus, Chevrolet Monte Carlo, and Pontiac Grand Prix of today arise from 50 years of development of the American sedan as a racing machine. But they are not nearly as fast as the unrestricted Ford Thunderbird or Chevrolet Monte Carlo of 20 years ago, and they wouldn't last a minute driving across the deeply rutted dirt tracks of stock car racing's youth. "Today they race on highways," Tim Flock once recalled. "Back then, we had plowed fields." This is the story of the sport and its machines. Growth was slow at first, but took off with the cars – from the Hudson Hornets and Olds 88s to the Fords, Chevrolets, and Pontiacs of today. It is a story of the drivers, too, and of the fabled arenas such as Darlington, Daytona, and Talladega.

THE HISTORY OF STOCK CAR RACING

Win on Sunday, sell on Monday. We identify with the family Ford,
Chevy, or Dodge. Because everyone has a car or truck, we ride
the banked speedway tracks along with the likes of Richard Petty,
Dale Earnhardt, and Jeff Gordon on Sunday afternoons.
That is the beauty and lure of stock car racing.

The evolution of the stock car as race car is one of revolution, risk taking, seemingly ridiculous folly, and radical notions. The idea that one machine on four wheels could go faster than another fueled more than one argument, even in the early days of automobiles. As cars became faster and better, those who drove them became bolder and more curious. In cars built for basic transportation, men raced from Paris to Rouen, France, in 1894, sparking an idea that would quickly cross the Atlantic. By 1896, the Rhode Island State Fair Association had turned the Narragansett Park horse track into an auto racing landscape, and fast cars began going in circles and turning left, a journey that has lasted more than a century.

On the hard-packed sand of Florida's Atlantic shore, at Daytona Beach and Ormond Beach, the arrival of the 20th century brought a revolution in motoring. The wide beaches provided the perfect surface for high-speed runs in the somewhat experimental automobiles of the day, and rich gentlemen who came to the area to escape the frigid northern winters soon found themselves in friendly competition. They ran up and down the beach in events they called land speed record runs, challenging the clock and each other in straight-line races. These competitions took on the flavor of a festival over the years, and soon thousands gathered on adjacent sand dunes to watch these vehicles test the limits of horsepower and endurance. The speed runs kept both Daytona and Ormond in the spotlight for years, but the era ended in 1935 when the quest for more speed moved west to the Bonneville Salt Flats in Utah. The loss of the speed shows opened the door for the next era in Daytona's motorsport history, and it was a grand one, indeed.

One interested spectator at the last land-speed session in March 1935 was Bill France, an auto mechanic who had relocated from Washington, D.C. Knowing something about fast cars (he had been racing his own since the mid-1920s), France settled

▲ BARNEY OLDFIELD

The great Barney Oldfield, who set many records in the early years of speed trials at Daytona Beach, Florida, raced his Lightning Benz from a standing start to a one-mile record of 88.845 mph in 1910.

◄ ROCKET RACER

Louis Ross drove the Stanley Rocket to victory on Daytona Beach, Florida, in 1905. His car had temendous acceleration provided by two small steam engines that controlled each rear wheel.

in Daytona Beach by chance but was quickly drawn to the competition on the shore. After Daytona lost the speed runs, worried city officials sought a quick replacement. They came up with an odd hybrid racecourse using the beach and the parallel pavement of Highway A1A a few yards away to form a temporary paper clip-shaped track. The American Automobile Association (AAA) ran its first race on the Daytona Beach-Road course in March 1936, and France, excited by the concept, entered and finished fifth. The first race was not a financial success, but France took over promotional duties and turned the event into a plus for the community over the next few years. By the time World War II put a halt to most auto racing, he had turned the Beach-Road course concept into a very popular and competitive attraction for both racers and spectators.

After the war, racing resumed on the beach, and stories of grand times and high speeds there began to attract daredevil drivers all over the East Coast. In the years before World War II, ragged dirt tracks had sprouted near small towns and at fairgrounds across

▲ ORIGINAL DAYTONA COURSE

Daytona Beach, Florida's famed Beach-Road course was a 4.1-mile oval with a slight dogleg on the paved stretch that remains Highway A1A. During an incoming tide, racing was particularly tricky.

much of the country, and men returning from the war filled them with 1930s modified jalopies in the post-war era. The mountainous areas of the western Carolinas and northern Georgia were hotbeds for raw-edged racing, in part because the established illegal moonshine whiskey culture of the region had bred a collection of fast-driving delivery men who could run the back roads with skill and authority.

▼ WORLD CENTER OF SPEED

Two early stars of the speed runs posed in front of the Ormond Garage before the 1905 meet. Officially called the Stanley Rocket, the Stanley Steamer (No. 4) driven by Louis Ross won all the head-to-head races. But Herbert L. Bowden became the first American to top 100 mph in the "Flying Dutchman" Mercedes.

France promoted several races in the Southeast in 1946 and developed a loosely organized association of racers with the idea of scheduling a series of events and naming a national champion.

STOCK CAR RACING ORGANIZES

Stock car racing was a ragged patchwork-in-progress in the late 1940s, a wayward and unruly child looking for a parent. Races were run at crude dirt ovals cut from pastures or wasteland, and promised purses were sometimes pocketed by the promoter. Several groups tried to organize racing. The American Automobile Association, then the sanctioning body for the Indianapolis 500 for open-wheel cars, also scheduled stock car races in the 1930s, many in California. Drivers were allowed minor modifications, but the AAA version of the stock car was generally a bare-bones road car. They did allow a second rider – a mechanic, in cars during the 1930s. The Central States Racing Association ran stock car races in the Midwest in the 1940s, while Boundbrook, New Jersey, was headquarters for the Eastern Stock Car Circuit in the same period. In 1947, France operated what was then called the National Championship Stock Car Circuit (NCSCC), which ran races at a variety of sites, including Greensboro and North Wilkesboro, North Carolina; Birmingham, Alabama; Greenville and Columbia, South Carolina; and Trenton, New Jersey. He named a point champion – Fonty Flock, one of three racing Flock brothers. Ed Samples, Red Byron, Bob Flock,

▲ **FRANCE BEFORE NASCAR**

Bill France entered the inaugural race on the Beach-Road course in 1936. He finished fifth in the AAA-sponsored event, and won it four years later.

and Buddy Shuman were other top guns in the series, which advertising described as "the fastest growing auto racing sport in the U.S.A." There was a big beating heart at the center of this new sport, for the men who drove the first lightning laps on the old dirt tracks were mavericks of the first degree, wild and footloose adventurers who loved the speed, the danger, and all the attendant fuss.

THE DAREDEVIL DRIVERS

The early days of semi-organized stock car racing provided playgrounds for men like James Swayne Pritchett (known as Swayne), a Georgia mountaineer who found fast cars and competition too tempting to refuse. Pritchett had run a few restaurants and sold used cars now and then and eventually became involved in almost any money-making activity In the years after World War II, young men returning home were suddenly wild and free, and, in the hill country north of Atlanta, they were often found in fast cars. Pritchett fell in with them and, by 1947, was racing a hot 1939 Ford coupe at every opportunity.

"He had a lot of ambition, and he was good at driving," remembered Tommy Irvin, who raced against Pritchett on the rural dirt ovals in Georgia and the Carolinas. "He was a natural. Back at that

◄ **HIGHLY MODIFIED**

Altered Ford coupes – usually the 1934, 1937, and 1939 models – became the foundation of Modified racing after World War II. This Ford, driven by Lewis Marshall, had an extended front frame as added protection for the radiator.

▲ **BOUNCING ACROSS THE RUTS**

John Rutherford (No. 29) drove his Auburn boattail speedster through the rutted north turn of the 1936 race at Daytona Beach, Florida.

time, there wasn't anything but dirt roads, and he learned to drive pretty good on them."

Pritchett's car, like many in those days, was a rebuilt '39 Ford rescued from former use as a family car. Refitted with minor modifications and its engine juiced with all the shade-tree mechanic knowledge available, it was an unrefined but powerful jalopy capable of remarkable speeds. Unfortunately, it was unpredictable in the often dangerous arena of fledgling dirt-track racing. It was as close to a "stock car" as any racer would be. Safety modifications were minimal. A safety belt secured with a steel cable was the only significant protection inside a speeding bullet on dirt tracks that often were so ragged that cars lost wheels in the ruts. On a late-spring weekend in only his second year of racing, Pritchett won a race and lost his life in the same moment, sudden and stark testimony to the thrilling yet sometimes brutally violent early days of a sport whose dangerous dark side would be tamed far too slowly to save some of its pioneers.

Although his racing career spanned only 1947 and the early months of 1948, Pritchett built a reputation as one of the best of the daredevil bunch of drivers who made Atlanta and its environs a sort of central hub for stock car racing in its infancy. Of 91 drivers listed in the point standings of Bill France's NCSCC organization in 1947, Pritchett ranked 17th. The fact that Pritchett's racing career ended abruptly on May 16, 1948, on a small dirt track near his hometown of Cornelia, Georgia, tells much about the state of the sport in those rough-and-tumble days and of the unusual men who populated it.

The race was at Jefferson Speedway, a half-mile dirt oval near Jefferson, Georgia. In car No. 17, on a track where he had run many laps, Pritchett breezed to victory. After sweeping under the checkered flag, he continued full bore toward the first turn, a stuck accelerator apparently turning his car into a missile. Pritchett's Ford hit another car that was already slowing after the finish. He struck it at full speed, shot into the air, and rolled over. The impact of the crash snapped the cable linked to Pritchett's seat belt and, as the car flipped, Pritchett was thrown from the vehicle. The car landed on his chest. He died of massive bleeding and internal injuries.

Swayne Pritchett, dead at age 26, left two sons and a daughter. They knew little of their father's racing exploits, having been shielded from the often unsavory nature of the sport at his own insistence.

▲ **DRAG RACING GETS A JUMP START**

Drag racing also organized in the early 1950s with the formation of the National Hot Rod Association by Wally Parks.

C. L. Pritchett, the younger son, was just five when his father died. By the late 1960s, however, the sport had drawn him in, and he became one of the top touring dirt-track drivers of his day, a tough and determined racer who realized many of the victories his father didn't live to chase. More than 50 years later, the track where Swayne Pritchett ran his last race is lifeless and windswept in the winter wind. There has been no racing there for many years. The sport has moved on.

The men on the front lines of early stock car racing were much like their machines – rugged, unrefined, and strong but vulnerable.

Everett "Cotton" Owens was from Spartanburg, South Carolina, a typical small Southern town that later would become a hotbed for motorsport. He had the racing bug by the late 1930s, years before he had a race car or even a legitimate place to run it. He already had the fever before World War II, and after the war he returned home to rebuild his life. For the next half-century, much of his time would be connected to cars and racing. He took a job at a local junkyard and was there the day a racer in trouble – Gober Sosebee – stopped by. Sosebee had crashed a car at a race in Richmond, Virginia, and needed a replacement body for that Saturday's race at the Piedmont Interstate Fairgrounds half-mile dirt track in Spartanburg.

Owens welded a new center section onto the car. Talking to Sosebee, one of the best drivers in the Atlanta area, and working on a race car gave Owens the push he needed to take the next step. He and several friends got together and rebuilt a wrecked 1937 Ford coupe they rescued from the junkyard. They pulled the engine and replaced it with a 1946 model, gaining a chunk of horsepower. They tinkered with the rear end gearing, put in a bigger radiator, and hauled it across the state line to a dirt track near Hendersonville, North Carolina. Other than those few changes, it was basically a stock car. "About the only other thing we did was chain the doors together with a bolt holding the chain links so the doors wouldn't come open," Owens said. He drove the car that day in Hendersonville, won his heat race, and went on to finish second in the main event. He had begun his racing career, but there was still much for him to learn.

▲ **1936 INAUGURAL WINNER**

Milt Marion won the first race on the Beach-Road course at Daytona Beach, Florida, in a Ford convertible coupe.

Stock car racing in the Southeast in the year after World War II generally meant short dirt-track competition between 1930s jalopies, mostly Fords, retooled with any improvements the drivers and mechanics could improvise. An article in the January 1948 issue of *Speed Age* magazine gave some tips on preparing a 1939 Ford coupe for racing. Among the suggestions was the removal of inside door handles and window cranks because "all of these items are aimed directly at you when you are flipping, so they cannot harm you if they are not there." Many preparation changes in those years came from the influences of the car culture of southern California, where speed-happy young men were building shiny street rods with modified carburetors and every speed device imaginable. They began installing two or three carburetors along with dual intake manifolds, different ignition systems, and whatever else they could think of to increase a car's speed.

In that vibrant atmosphere, these teenagers could be found buzzing the beaches in street rods, gunning their monster engines at the downtown stoplights, and creating a brash, new culture built around their fast, hopped-up cars.

Among the first to see where racing and hot cars were headed was an Atlanta-based mechanic named Louis "Red" Vogt, who was to become one of the most influential car builders of the early years of stock car racing. His Atlanta shop ("Open 24 Hours," the sign out front read) built high-performance cars for both the northern Georgia whiskey-running operations and for men trying to gain the upper hand in the first days of racing for pay on the bumpy dirt tracks across the Southeast.

▲ **STONE, WOODS, AND COOK**

The driver is just part of the equation, a point emphasized by the famed Stone, Woods, and Cook drag racing team – which was also a pioneer multi-racial enterprise. The caucasian Doug Cook drove the 1941 blown gas Willys coupe for African-American owners – crewmen Fred Stone and Tim Woods.

Vogt's skills attracted the interest of Atlanta businessman Raymond Parks, a sharp operator with money to spend and friends who wanted to help him spend it in racing. Parks wrote checks for cars Vogt put together, and daredevil drivers like Roy Hall, Lloyd Seay, Red Byron, and Bob Flock rode them to win after win. Parks was a key figure in the racing community taking shape in the postwar years. A car owner who took pride in both the performance and appearance of his vehicles, he spared no expense in buying the best cars and keeping them in top shape.

Men like Owens and Parks were racing along at the very heart of the Southern stock car culture when, near the midpoint of the century, a change took place that was to profoundly affect the sport. Up to then, racing in the South primarily meant competition between the aging, retooled 1930s cars that had been rescued from their junkyard oblivion. The emergence of NASCAR, with new ideas from founder Bill France Sr., and the new peacetime technologies, were destined to change the face of the sport dramatically.

THE BIRTH OF NASCAR

Little by little, the sport was coming alive. "Racing those 1934 and 1937 Ford coupes was about all we knew," Cotton Owens said. "Everybody wanted them because they were so much lighter and ran so good. On short tracks, that was the answer: the lighter you were, the faster you ran." The old Fords had proven themselves as first-class whiskey-running cars, too, until Bill France roared in and changed the emphasis of the sport. After enjoying some modest success promoting auto races on the Daytona Beach course and at short tracks across the Southeast, he

15

took a giant step. In a series of meetings with drivers, promoters, and interested hangers-on during December 1947, France formed the National Association for Stock Car Auto Racing (NASCAR). By 1948, France was running successful races under the NASCAR name, still using the "Modified" 1930s-era cars that were the first generation of racing vehicles in the Southeast.

He had bigger ideas, however. The United States, at peace and with a growing economy, was becoming an automotive society, and France saw the future of motorsport linked to the American highway. He felt he could sell a sport featuring fearless drivers competing in cars more or less identical to those on highways, and thus was born NASCAR's Strictly Stock series, now known as NASCAR Winston Cup. The plan was simple: Take "showroom" American-built cars, modify them only slightly, and race them on the racetracks of the day.

WINSTON CUP RACING BEGINS

The first test of France's plan was a 150-mile race on June 19, 1949, at the Charlotte Speedway near what is now Interstate 85 in Charlotte, North Carolina. France announced a $5,000 purse, and promoted the event with emphasis on the "strictly stock" nature of cars that would run in the event.

Big, new, American-built family sedans would be raced this way for the very first time. Interest was high. Early on race morning, thousands of spectators were already in the vicinity of the

▲ **LIMITED ACCESS**
NASCAR moved to improve all aspects of stock car racing, including credentialing of officials and media.

speedway. By the green flag, a throng of about 13,000 ringed the dirt track. They came to see the best racers of the day – drivers like Tim Flock, Lee Petty, and Jim Paschal – participate in this new undertaking. The cars were virtually all showroom-black sedans, with their headlights and grilles taped over in futile attempts to protect their new bodies against the rocks sent flying from the racing surface.

As they raced into the first left turn of a new era, dust soared into the air, and it enveloped the track the rest of the way. At race's end, Glenn Dunnaway of nearby Gastonia rolled under the checkered flag first. A postrace inspection showed that Dunnaway's 1947 Ford was not exactly "showroom stock," however, for it had been modified with heavy support springs in the rear – a change typical of the moonshine-running cars of the day, which carried big loads in their trunks. Dunnaway's car was disqualified, and the first victory of what would later become NASCAR's Winston Cup series went to Jim Roper, a Kansan who had driven his 1949 Lincoln on an unlikely journey to the race and then followed Dunnaway across the finish line.

The race had brought the first in what would be a long history of controversies to the series, but it also certified France's belief that fans would be attracted in throngs to a style of racing that featured cars very similar to those driven on American streets and highways. It was a natural, and fans immediately began to build alliegances to their favorite automakers France confidently began to build on the new concept, adding races up and down the East Coast and

▼ **NASCAR BRANCHES OUT**
NASCAR fielded a Speedway division in 1952–53. Stock car engines ran in Indy-type chassis. Top drivers, including Fireball Roberts here, tried out open-wheel Champ Car racing.

spreading west into new territories. France also retained the unique flavor of Daytona racing by scheduling several events on the Beach-Road course and continuing to attract large crowds to what remains one of the unique racing landscapes of the 21st century. The oceanside course hosted its last stock car races during the 1958 season, the year before France opened the mammoth and revolutionary Daytona International Speedway a few miles inland.

▲ **PLAYING IN THE DIRT**

Curtis Turner plowed through the dirt of the south turn and headed toward the beach during the 1950 race at Daytona Beach, Florida. Turner drove a 1949 Lincoln.

SPECTACULAR SPILL

A favorite spectator spot at Daytona Beach was inside the south turn. Drivers turned in from the Highway A1A asphalt onto the sand, tried to gain traction quickly, and roared up the beach. They accelerated out of that corner as quickly as they could, and when the tide started coming in, some of them ran out into the surf. It was dangerous for spectators as well as drivers. People would lean out over the highway to get a look at the cars and then move back as they approached.

The outside of the south turn quickly became a graveyard for cars as drivers misjudged their speed coming down the road and entering the turn, even though stripes had been painted on the highway to provide a suggested braking point. Unfortunate competitors who erred here overshot the curve and flipped over into a

▼ **DURABLE BUT UGLY**

The Nash Ambassador was an unlikely race car. Big and underpowered, its one strength was its ability to grind through the dirt-track ruts that broke the wheel assemblies and suspensions of many other vehicles.

pit behind a sand bank. The beach course attracted drivers from across the country. One, Russ Truelove, drove south from his home in Waterbury, Connecticut, in 1956 to run the beach race in a brand-new two-door Mercury hardtop he had just ordered from the Lincoln-Mercury dealership where he was employed as the service manager. He put in a roll bar and painted and numbered the car before driving it to Daytona. During the race, he tried to pass Jim Reed, one of the sport's top short-track drivers, as they neared the north turn. "I thought I'd try to get him on the inside," Truelove said. But he got caught in the softer sand, his front wheel dug in, and he couldn't correct it. The 1956 Mercury required five full turns of the steering wheel to make a full turn of the wheels. The car started fishtailing and eventually flipped into the air.

Truelove wasn't hurt, but spectacular photos of the wreck appeared in *Life* magazine, displaying his violent ride to the world. He would soon become a celebrity of sorts, but he had a new problem for the moment. He had driven all the way down the East Coast in a car that had been reduced to a crumpled, undriveable heap. Fortunately for Truelove, a man from a Ford dealership in Hartford, Connecticut just happened to be in the area, repossessing cars. "We took two of the repossessed cars off his hauler and put my car up on top," said Truelove. "I drove home in one of the repossessed cars." Such was often the lot of those men trying desperately to make a go of it in the early days of stock car racing. The sport, however, was on the verge of great changes. The reach of its new popularity began to expand from the Southeastern roots of racing's prewar years. This enthusiasm for racing was fed by the nation's growing peacetime prosperity and its love affair with the newer, more powerful cars being produced for a burgeoning population of drivers.

FAST DRIVERS, FASTER TRACKS

Among those racing on the beach, and in many events in NASCAR's first decade, was a young man from Daytona Beach, Florida, who had picked up the nickname "Fireball" from his youthful days as a pitcher on the baseball diamond. His real name was Glenn Roberts, and his exploits would help to put his sport in front of a much wider audience. Roberts was a friend of Marshall Teague, another Daytona Beach pioneer racer. They had raced on Florida tracks in the late 1940s and joined France's traveling road show when NASCAR began putting some structure under what had been a largely disorganized sport. Roberts became one of NASCAR's first star drivers. Smart, daring, personable, handsome, and tagged with a nickname that seemed perfect, he gave the sport an appealing new face.

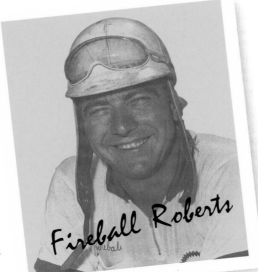

Fireball Roberts

◀ **FIRST SUPERSTAR**

The witty and outgoing Glenn "Fireball" Roberts was stock car racing's first national headliner. His 32 wins included four each at Daytona International Speedway and Darlington Raceway.

Men like Roberts, Herb Thomas, Curtis Turner, the Flock brothers (Tim, Fonty, Bob), Buck Baker, Junior Johnson, Lee Petty, Red Byron, and Jack Smith blazed new trails for NASCAR in the 1950s. They drove Hudson Hornets, Studebakers, Chrysler 300s, and Nash Ambassadors with abandon. Occasionally, as in Swayne Pritchett's case, the hard realities of racing's early years were fatal. Frank Arford died during a qualifying run at the Langhorne Speedway in 1953. Lou Figaro died in a crash during a race at North Wilkesboro, North Carolina, in 1954. Yet another accident at the same track killed John McVitty in 1956, and Clint McHugh and Thomas Priddy were killed at the Memphis-Arkansas Speedway, a very fast 1.5-mile dirt track, in 1956. Racers learned from each accident, but speed was picking up and safety measures were slow in coming.

THE FIFTIES

The 1950s opened and closed with two significant debuts for NASCAR, and included several other changes across the landscape of American stock car racing during the years in between.

▶ **THE TEAGUEMOBILE**

Marshall Teague posed with his Hudson Hornet after winning the 160-mile Daytona Beach Road Race on February 11, 1951. It was the first of 143 races won by the "Fabulous" Hornet.

Darlington Raceway, NASCAR's first paved track and its first superspeedway, opened September 4, 1950, accompanied by great curiosity and apprehension. Built by Darlington resident Harold Brasington with little more than a dream and a bulldozer, the track would host the first 500-mile race for NASCAR stockers, and the first competition on a paved surface. No one knew what to expect, and many doubted that the cars and drivers could last that long at the higher speeds.

Seventy-five cars started the race, and more than 20,000 fans crowded into the new facility to watch what would happen. The first lap was chaos of the first order. Dirt and dust clouds filled the air. The drivers couldn't see anything. Many just ran off blindly into the first turn and tried to keep their cars running. The day's major problem, however, was foreseen by very few. The cars' high speeds and the track's surface resulted in excessive tire wear, and drivers were popping into the pits for fresh tires with alarming frequency. Few teams were prepared for this, and some sent runners into the infield to remove tires from spectators' cars and haul them to the pits for use in the race. Winner Johnny Mantz, the slowest qualifier for the race, finished first by pacing himself and his car, going slower than most other drivers early in the race but also preserving his tires and needing fewer pit stops. A veteran racer who had learned the trade driving midgets on the Pacific coast in the 1930s and '40s, the Californian had beaten the Southern boys in their first superspeedway extravaganza.

Street drag racers found a legitimate home in 1951 when Wally Parks founded the National Hot Rod Association. The NHRA held its first race in April 1953 in the Los Angeles County Fairgrounds parking lot in Pomona, California. Half a century later, the sanctioning body retains its ties to the street-rod days of the 1950s within its Funny Car class, a lightning-fast division for cars with stock shells. The International Hot Rod Association joined the mix in 1970. Founded by Tennessean Larry Carrier, who also developed the Bristol Motor Speedway at Bristol, Tennessee, the IHRA provided another tier, and another collection of dragways, for straight-line racers. IHRA developed several divisions around the concept of the pure stock car, including the Funny Car.

Other sanctioning bodies were forming, as well. John Marcum, a former NASCAR official, started the Midwest Association for Race Cars (MARC) in Toledo, Ohio, in 1953. Ten years later, MARC, by then a thriving entity, was sanctioning a 35-race schedule in 17 states and had changed its name to the Automobile Racing Club of America. ARCA continues racing today, its history as a wide-ranging, versatile organization including the early-career driving of drivers like Mark Martin, Benny Parsons, Kyle Petty, Tim Richmond, Davey Allison, Ernie Irvan, Jeremy Mayfield, and Alan Kulwicki. Several of these men had also scored victories in the International Motor Contest Association (IMCA), which had crowned champions long before NASCAR and the United States Auto Club (USAC) came along. IMCA's history dates to a race at the Michigan State Fairgrounds in 1915.

In 1955, the American Automobile Association stopped sanctioning auto racing altogether. The decision left a vacuum that soon resulted in the establishment of the United States Auto Club, which took over running the Indianapolis 500 and also began sanctioning, among other motorsport series, a stock car racing division.

▲ POWER OF PERFECTION

Carl Kiekhaefer, known for his stable of Chrysler 300s, also campaigned a Dodge Coronet. Frank Mundy stood beside the D-500 that ran in the Convertible Division in 1956.

Although open-wheel cars were USAC's image, the organization developed a respected Midwestern-based stock car series with a number of winning drivers who would come to greater fame in other racing series. The list includes A. J. Foyt, Jack Bowsher, Roger McCluskey, Al Unser Sr., Norm Nelson, and Don White.

If Darlington opened NASCAR's superspeedway era, Daytona accelerated it. With development crowding the formerly wide-open spaces used to form the Daytona Beach-Road course, Bill France looked west for a new place to race. After much complicated planning and considerable financial maneuvering, he made the gigantic Daytona International Speedway a reality, opening the 2.5-mile track in 1959. The speedway, a new animal for stock car racers because of the staggering speeds it produced, revolutionized the sport. Stock car racing, which had not had a track to rival the size and spectacular presence of the famed Indianapolis Motor Speedway, finally had its crown jewel. Daytona opened with a wide, superfast racing surface and long, sweeping grandstands that offered the spectators tremendous views of what would become one of the most famous front stretches in auto racing. Some drivers, upon seeing the track for the first time, were shocked at the new landscape for racing, and few

▲ IMITATING INDY

The field started three-abreast for the first Southern 500 in 1950 at Darlington Raceway, South Carolina, because that was the way they started 500-mile races at the Indianapolis Motor Speedway.

of them felt any doubt about the speeds that would result. The sight of the spacious racing surface led the veteran dirt-track racer Fireball Roberts to observe wryly that "even a gorilla can drive here."

The first race on the track, the inaugural Daytona 500, ran February 22, 1959. The final laps matched Lee Petty's Oldsmobile and the Ford of Johnny Beauchamp. Petty edged Beauchamp by a few feet in one of the closest races in stock car history. Beauchamp initially was awarded the victory, but three days of studying photographs and film of the finish convinced France that Petty had, indeed, reached the finish line first.

Daytona's success sparked more growth. In the 1960s, tracks opened at Charlotte and Rockingham, North Carolina; Atlanta, Georgia; Talladega, Alabama; Bristol, Tennessee; Dover, Delaware; and Brooklyn, Michigan. The sport was moving away

▶ REMARKABLE FINISH

The photo finish of the first Daytona 500 in 1959 attracted national attention. Johnny Beauchamp was originally declared the winner, but photographs reviewed days later proved Lee Petty (No. 42 inside the lapped car of Joe Weatherly) won the race.

from the short tracks that had given it life and was attracting throngs to superspeedways specifically built to showcase the speed and endurance of cars that were becoming more sophisticated.

SPEED AND SAFETY

NASCAR lost its first superstar in 1964, a year that stock car racing was forced to face a number of safety issues. Fireball Roberts, a popular racer whose dynamic style had given the sport a new nuance, ran his final race in the World 600 on May 24 at the Charlotte Motor Speedway.

On the eighth lap of the race, Ned Jarrett and Junior Johnson collided in the second turn, starting a wreck that eventually involved Roberts, whose car spun into the inside wall and flipped. Leaking fuel started a fire in Roberts' car, and an ugly plume of black smoke formed over the second turn as Jarrett jumped from his car and ran to Roberts. Still trapped inside the car, Roberts said, "Oh, my God, Ned, help me. I'm on fire." Outside the car, Jarrett helped Roberts remove his charred uniform. Roberts, burned critically, remained hospitalized in Charlotte until he died on July 2 from a blood infection. He is buried in a quiet cemetery in Daytona Beach. In the distance, on race days, the sound of stock car thunder can be heard from the speedway where Roberts once raced.

Roberts' death was the stark centerpiece of a dark period for auto racing. From January 1964 to January 1965, four NASCAR drivers – Jimmy Pardue, Billy Wade, Joe Weatherly, and Roberts – died in racing accidents. In addition, IndyCar drivers Eddie Sachs and Dave MacDonald were killed in the 1964 Indianapolis 500.

▲ **BUILT FOR SAFETY**

One of the first safety innovations in stock car racing was the welded support to protect the driver in side impact collisions.

Stock car racing reacted to the problems. The next two years saw two major developments: the creation of a rubber fuel cell to prevent fires in accidents, and the invention of the tire inner liner, which gave an extra layer of protection when the outside surface of a tire failed.

The 1960s also was a watershed decade in other ways. NASCAR was moving away from racing cars built on Detroit assembly lines and toward specially-designed motorsport vehicles. A standard chassis was developed, creating a more or less universal piece upon which teams constructed the rest of the race car. Specialty shops catered to teams looking to buy race-ready cars, and the sport steadily drove away from its grassroots "race what's on the street" foundation. Now, even though the fans still root for favorite makes such as Ford and Chevrolet, the Winston Cup cars of the present era have become barely recognizable as specific car models. Their lines are curved and tweaked to provide the smoothest aerodynamic shapes, front air dams and rear spoilers are added for speed and stability, and fender areas are enlarged for the specially manufactured racing tires. These sleek, made-to-race vehicles are now generations removed from the top-heavy, bulky, "strictly stock" steel monsters driven by racing's first-generation drivers of the early 1950s.

EXPANSION YEARS

As NASCAR gained steam and spread its top series to bigger speedways, new sanctioning bodies formed to feed America's appetite for more stock car racing. Some became feeder systems for the upper levels of NASCAR; others built their own driver and fan bases and survived on their own, and some did both.

▲ **TOPS DOWN**

Stock cars come in all shapes and sizes. From 1955 to 1959, NASCAR ran a Convertible division shown here racing at Darlington Raceway.

The Sports Car Club of America and the International Motor Sports Association, both known primarily for competition matching sleek sports cars and high-tech powerful prototype racers, jumped into the stock car racing game. The SCCA developed the popular Trans-American Sedan Championship in 1966, gave it a sexier name (Trans-Am) and then unleashed drivers like Mark Donohue, Parnelli Jones, and George Follmer in Camaros, Mustangs, Challengers, and Barracudas. The series continued with major and minor tweaks through the years, and, in 1997, recorded one of the most amazing achievements in motorsport history as Tom Kendall won 11 straight races on the way to his fourth Trans-Am championship. IMSA was formed in 1969 by John Bishop, who developed a Grand Touring (GT) division for stock sports cars in 1971 and introduced numerous series over the years that matched American-built stockers like Mustangs, Camaros, and Firebirds with foreign-made entries.

Promoter Rex Robbins founded the American Speed Association in 1968 and scheduled its first stock car event in July of that year. ASA grew each year and, in 1973, developed a platform for a national touring series, expanding from its Midwestern base. A young driver named Darrell Waltrip won the inaugural National Circuit of Champions race. Rusty Wallace, Mike Eddy, Bob Senneker, Johnny Benson, and Mark Martin also built solid foundations for their own successful careers in ASA racing.

NATIONAL EXPOSURE

After steady growth through the 1960s, NASCAR reached a crossroads in 1972. The R. J. Reynolds Tobacco Company had signed on in 1971 as sponsor of the Grand National (the name France had given his featured series in its second season) and wanted the tour to be made up of bigger, more select events. For the '72 season, most shorter tracks were dropped and the schedule was trimmed to 31 races. RJR put thousands of dollars – later, millions – into a driver point fund that paid at the end of the season, and new emphasis was placed on winning the seasonal championship, renamed the NASCAR Winston Cup.

The next big step after RJR's sponsorship commitment was a new partnership with television, which had virtually ignored stock car racing for years. Little live racing was broadcast, and the three networks couldn't be sold on broadcasting a major race from start to finish. ABC signed on to show the concluding segment of the 1976 Daytona 500, however, a decision that would prove to change the networks' view of NASCAR racing forever.

RIVALRIES

Stock car racing has seen some titanic rivalries over the years. In perhaps the greatest of these contests, David Pearson and Richard Petty fought like feuding strongmen for control of NASCAR's high ground in the 1960s and 1970s. They had similar backgrounds but markedly different styles. Each grew up in hard times in small-town Carolina communities; each took to short-track racing like moths to flame. Upon arriving on the NASCAR stage (Petty in 1958, Pearson in 1960), however, they traveled very different roads.

Petty was the ultimate racing celebrity – tall and handsome, with a big smile and a personality that drew fans by the thousands. He quickly became an ambassador for racing – a walking, talking fountain of enthusiasm for a sport still rough around the edges that needed a new clean-cut image to position itself closer to the mainstream. Petty was the right man at the right time. In the 1960s, he drove himself to victory after victory on the tracks and carried the sport to new heights of popularity. Soon, he was King Richard.

Pearson, shy and hesitant around those he did not know, was Petty's polar opposite. He stayed in the shadows, a man who could drive as well as anyone but who didn't care for the extra packaging that came with the job. He wasn't mean or arrogant, but simply uncomfortable in the spotlight and preferred to keep quiet and let his talent do the talking.

▲ **GREATEST RIVALRY**

David Pearson and Richard Petty (No. 43) battled for a quarter of a century. They ran 1-2 a record 63 times, including the famous 1976 Daytona 500 battle won by Pearson.

These two giants of the sport met head-on in February, 1976. They came to Daytona clearly the top drivers of the day. Petty drove the slick red and blue No. 43 Dodge that had made him famous. Pearson was in the regal maroon, white, and gold No. 21 Mercury that practically oozed the sort of class Glen and Leonard Wood built into all of their racers. In that season's Daytona 500, before a huge national television audience and a throng of disbelieving witnesses at Daytona International Speedway, they staged a battle that rocked the foundation of stock car racing.

It was almost expected in those days for Winston Cup races to enter the final laps with Pearson and Petty in a race of their own. In fact, they finished 1-2 a record 63 times. In the glow of that Daytona Sunday, it would be so again. Petty raced into the lead with 13 laps remaining, Pearson following. Adding spark to the occasion was ABC television, which had joined the race in progress and was sending the final laps across the country live.

The last lap found the rivals alone at the front, Petty leading under the white flag, Pearson in his shadow. First Pearson

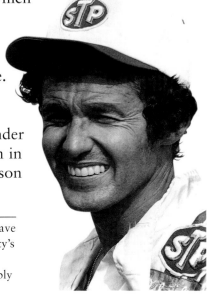

▶ **THE KING**

Because the racing seasons have been shortened, Richard Petty's record of 200 NASCAR Winston Cup wins is probably beyond reach.

▲ EYES OF A NATION

Dale Jarrett conducted one of many postrace television interviews after winning his second Daytona 500 in 1996.

passed Petty, then, in the final turn of the race, Petty had tried to pass Pearson by going low, but he slipped as their cars rolled through the turn side by side and struck Pearson's car. They both hit the outside wall, Petty careening down the track out of control, Pearson bouncing off the concrete, across the pavement and onto the grass separating the track from the pit road. The grandstands erupted with cheers, easily audible over the roar of engines a few feet away. Then, 23-year-old Eddie Wood, the son of Pearson's team owner, heard Pearson's calm voice in his headset. "Where's Richard?" he asked. Wood told him Petty's car was sitting in the grass and couldn't get started. Pearson said, "I'm coming." And he did. At the moment of the crash impact, Pearson had depressed the clutch on his car, keeping the engine alive despite the battering the car had absorbed. He slammed into gear, pulled off the apron and onto the bottom of the racing surface, and limped across the finish line at about 20 mph to win the most dramatic Daytona 500 in history. Petty's Dodge was a crippled mess in the grass. His crew raced across pit road to try to push the car, which was a clear rules violation, but it mattered little. Pearson had won.

This was big stuff for stock car racing. ABC, which had delayed its coverage of the Winter Olympics to show the 500 finish and its aftermath, had stepped into untested territory, committing live time to a key race and to an audience still largely unknown. Long enamored of the so-called "stick and ball sports," television flirted hesitantly with

▼ THEY CAN FLY

Paul Simon went airborne in his Ford Ranger during a SCORE off-road race in Baja California, Mexico. Paul and brother David won SCORE titles in Ford pickups.

auto racing for years, showing only portions of events and using motorsport as a sort of filler on anthology programs such as ABC's *Wide World of Sports*. NASCAR, now the holder of a new $2.4 billion television contract, then had to lobby for TV exposure. It was a hard sell.

The 1976 Daytona 500 was a key element in changing that perspective. Suddenly, NASCAR had a product to peddle. Three years later, it cashed its chips in style. In yet another Daytona spectacle, national television cameras, this time owned by CBS, beamed the 1979 race nationwide from start to

their grievances when Bobby Allison, Donnie's brother, stopped his car at the wreck site. Words were exchanged, and Bobby Allison and Yarborough wound up in a brief fight sent across the country by CBS cameras. The '79 race now is viewed by many as a turning point in NASCAR racing. With much of the country watching, stock car racing's most intense elements – the strong will to win, and the willingness of some drivers to go beyond the ragged edge to get there – had been put on display.

Television also had a key role in the growth of another popular form of stock car racing, the

▲ **CLOSE-QUARTER DRILLS**

Four-time champion Mark Martin pushed the Dodge Sebring driven by Jeff Burton to the inside of Dale Earnhardt during the 2000 International Race of Champions heat at Daytona International Speedway.

finish, a first. The gamble paid off big. The race came down to another last-lap struggle, with Donnie Allison leading Cale Yarborough down the long backstretch. Yarborough shot to the inside to make what probably would have been the winning pass. Allison turned low to block him, and they bumped into each other, eventually crashing through the third turn and dropping off the high banking onto the track apron. Petty, running well behind them in third place, saw the door open and raced through. He took the checkered flag to win. Meanwhile, Allison and Yarborough, both steamed by the turn of events, were beginning to address

International Race of Champions. First conceived as a made-for-TV series, with short sprint races designed to fit into a one-hour broadcast space, IROC was born in 1973. The concept was simple yet dynamic: put twelve of the best race car drivers in the world into identically prepared cars and turn them loose on some of the country's best speedways. No one made the claim that the IROC champion was the best driver in the world, but many top drivers accepted invitations to the series, and its champions list boasted some of the greatest drivers on any race course: Mark Donohue, Bobby Unser, Cale Yarborough, A. J. Foyt, Al Unser,

Mario Andretti, Bobby Allison, Dale Earnhardt, Mark Martin, Davey Allison, and Rusty Wallace, among others. The first series featured Porsche Carerra RSR cars and was contested on road courses. Oval tracks were added the next year, and Chevrolet Camaros replaced the Porsches, as the series became more Americanized to suit the television audience. Over the years since its inception, the IROC became much more NASCAR-flavored, with Winston Cup-based chassis design and fields packed with the familiar names of NASCAR stars.

INTERNATIONAL COMPETITION

The 24 Hours of Le Mans, one of the world's marquee auto racing events, isn't normally associated with stock car racing. In 1976, that changed in a big way as stock cars invaded the famous Mulsanne straight. The occasion was a promotional coup by NASCAR kingpin Bill France, who brokered a deal that resulted in howling,

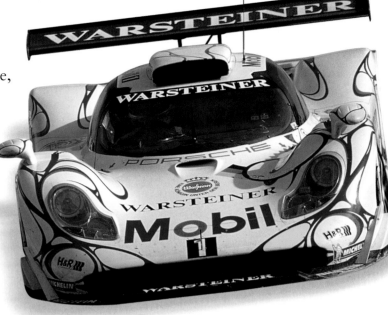

▲ **THE EXOTIC PROTOTYPE**

Europe has two widely different forms of stock car racing. Hybrid factory-backed machines like this are called prototypes. They appear in such international events as the 24 Hours of Le Mans.

growling stock cars, or at least a hybrid of the Winston Cup car, roaming the roads of Le Mans along with the sleek prototype sports cars of the era. Earlier that year, stock cars racing under the newly-coined Grand International name had participated in the 24 Hours of Daytona at Daytona International Speedway.

At Le Mans, the Fords of Junie Donlavey and Hershel McGriff were fitted with all manner of exotic modifications to make them fit the mold. In the same field with smaller, swifter, sportier cars, they had no chance of winning, of course. But it was a new spectacle – thundering stock cars unleashed on French soil. Enthusiastic French fans were intrigued by the sight of the big, novel racers Americans called the stock car, labelling Donlavey's car "Le Monster."

▼ **AROUND THE CLOCK**

The opening event of Speed Weeks each February at Daytona International Speedway is the 24 Hours of Daytona. The endurance sports car race is run on a road course that includes the third and fourth turns of the high-banked oval.

In the late 19th and early 20th centuries the roads of Europe had been host to some of the first auto racing in the world. Men in a variety of cars raced along country roads from Paris to Vienna and Paris to Madrid. In a race from Paris to Madrid in 1903, accidents claimed the lives of more than 20 drivers and spectators. When racing resumed after World War I, events were staged on short courses in and around the larger cities. Paris, Marseilles, Geneva, and Rome all ran events at one time or another. The appearance of the car they called "Le Monster" was little more than a novelty, a brief but welcome deviation, in the rich racing history of Europe.

▲ **STOCK TRUCKS**

With trucks becoming almost as popular as sedans with younger American drivers, NASCAR launched its Craftsman Truck Series in 1995.

THE MODERN ERA

The 1970s ended with Richard Petty's last big bang when he won the 1979 national championship for the seventh time, outgunning upstart Darrell Waltrip in the last race of the year. Arriving on the scene that season was the man who ultimately would assume Petty's place atop the stock car racing world. He was a tall refugee from the textile mill village of Kannapolis, North Carolina, named Dale Earnhardt. After building his reputation as a tough customer on the short tracks in Late Model Sportsman racing, Earnhardt worked his way into NASCAR Winston Cup competition and won the rookie of the year award in 1979. The next season, racing for owner Rod Osterlund, he captured five victories and his first NASCAR Winston Cup championship.

Earnhardt was a tough bump-and-run racer who would spark more than a few controversies in the ensuing years, and he quickly became the man to beat. He and Darrell Waltrip were the sport's big

guns in the 1980s as stock car racing moved along with more force – literally and figuratively. Television sent nearly every race to viewers across the country as speeds rose to unheard-of heights. Bill Elliott, who raced out of northern Georgia and into sudden prominence in the sport in the 1980s, took the speed gauge to its high point in 1987 with a 212-mph lap during his qualifying runs at Talladega. The same year, Bobby Allison had a frightening ride into the frontstretch fence at the same Alabama track, and this prompted officials to lower the speeds, first with smaller carburetors and later with carburetor restrictor plates that limited horsepower. The plates, heavily criticized by drivers, remain a favorite tool of NASCAR, which has instituted more restrictions every time speeds at the tour's two biggest tracks, Daytona and Talladega, climb toward 200 mph.

As the '80s rolled on, Waltrip, Earnhardt, and Elliott replaced Petty, Pearson, Yarborough, and Bobby Allison at the top. Allison, a hard-nosed racer in his own right, enjoyed rivalries with Petty and Waltrip and ended his career in 1988 with 84 wins and one NASCAR Winston Cup title. Yarborough retired that year, his victory total at 83, with three Winston Cup championships. Pearson left in 1986, second to Petty in career wins with 105.

Petty stayed until 1992. His 200th and last win came in 1984 at Daytona. Coincidentally, his last race, at Atlanta Motor Speedway that November, was the very first for the sport's next great superstar.

At a press conference on a January morning in 1992, H. A. "Humpy" Wheeler, Lowe's Motor Speedway promotional genius, stood at the microphone next to an impossibly young-looking new driver.

Wheeler was introducing Jeff Gordon to the national auto racing media. He talked about how legends like Richard Petty and A. J. Foyt come along about once per generation. He said he saw that sort of promise in Gordon, who looked young enough be on his way to the senior prom.

This was just another thing Wheeler was right about over the years. Gordon was a quick success in Busch Grand National racing, and wily NASCAR Winston Cup car owner Rick Hendrick lured the young racer onto his team and brought mechanic Ray Evernham along with him.

Gordon started racing at the age of five and had been a terror in the open-wheel sprints and midgets. He quickly adjusted to heavier cars. His first outing went unnoticed in the hoopla surrounding Petty's final race. He didn't remain in the shadows for long, however.

The young driver was a fresh face for NASCAR, an intense, handsome winner who came into stock car racing without the strong Southern short-track ties of many

▶ HAPPY CHAMPION

Jeff Gordon is the 11th driver in NASCAR Winston Cup history to win 50 races.

▲ MODERN RIVALS

The NASCAR Winston Cup Series was dominated in the 1990s by the Chevrolets driven by Dale Earnhardt, inside, and Jeff Gordon.

before him. Yet Gordon approached stock car racing with daring and authority, dispatching the veteran drivers with bold, split-second moves and winning some of the sport's biggest races during his first few years on the tour. He was the torch-bearer as NASCAR opened several new markets in the West, particularly in southern California; Las Vegas, Nevada; and Dallas-Fort Worth, Texas. He raced to victory as well in a spectacular debut in 1994 at the famed Indianapolis Motor Speedway, a venue which had previously been strictly limited to open-wheel cars. In 1995, only his third full season in NASCAR Winston Cup racing, Gordon won the series championship, then repeated the feat in both 1997 and 1998.

Gordon's three quick championships in the 1990s, added to another by his teammate, Terry Labonte, in 1996, established team owner Rick Hendrick as a major force in stock car racing. The Hendrick team's success had proved conclusively that the multicar team, a once-successful concept that had been scorned in stock car racing for years, could produce championships. Others saw the potential and quickly joined the movement, and a two-car system bore fruit once again in 1999 for car owner Robert Yates, a veteran engine builder with long ties to the sport. Yates, after years of struggle, finally had a won NASCAR Winston Cup championship with driver Dale Jarrett.

Other top drivers of the past 20 years included Rusty Wallace, who led a growing movement of impressive Midwesterners, and Alan Kulwicki, who beat the odds to win a championship with his own underfinanced team a few months before dying in a small plane crash on the way to a race at Bristol, Tennessee. Along with Kulwicki, two other top drivers lost to death in recent years were Davey Allison, son of Bobby Allison, and Neil Bonnett, like the Allisons a member of the Alabama Gang, a corps of drivers from the heart of Dixie who challenged the Carolinas-Georgia bunch for every piece of asphalt. Davey Allison won 19 races and built a huge fan following before his death from injuries suffered in a helicopter crash at Talladega in 1993. Bonnett, a winner 18 times in NASCAR Winston Cup racing, was killed in a crash during practice at Daytona in February 1994.

The Craftsman Truck series for American-made pickup trucks was launched at Phoenix International Raceway February 5, 1995. It quickly made stars of drivers like Ron Hornaday, Jack Sprague, and Mike Skinner, proving that the stock truck, like the stock car, could be a viable platform for racing, an idea already underlined by SCORE, which had established a successful off-road truck series.

NASCAR celebrated its golden anniversary throughout the 1998 season with a series of special events, spotlights on its past, and the naming of the 50 greatest drivers of its first half-century. As the surviving members of that select group, old-time pioneer drivers like Buck Baker, Junior Johnson, Herb Thomas, and Cotton Owens, as well as modern-era stars such as Dale Earnhardt, Jeff Gordon, Mark Martin, and Dale Jarrett, stood on the stage at Daytona Beach International Speedway to accept their awards, they represented a grand mix of daring drivers and wonderful race cars.

Over the past five decades, these men and their contemporaries had traveled the beaches of Florida, the red clay of the Carolinas, and the high-speed, banked asphalt of superspeedways like Talladega and Daytona. They had raced one another in cars ranging from the rebuilt junkyard jalopies of the 1930s and '40s to the sleek and powerful built-for-racing machines of the new millenium. Although their eras were vastly different, each had found success in a machine they called the stock car, a vehicle whose definition and look had changed immensely during the past half century but whose identity would always be based on how much thunder it carried into the first turn.

▼ **POETRY IN MOTION**

The Travis Carter pit crew swung into action on Jimmy Spencer's Ford Taurus during the Dura Lube 400 on February 21, 1999, at Rockingham, North Carolina. The first can of gas had already been dumped as tire changers tightened lug nuts with impact wrenches and the jack man prepared to drop the car.

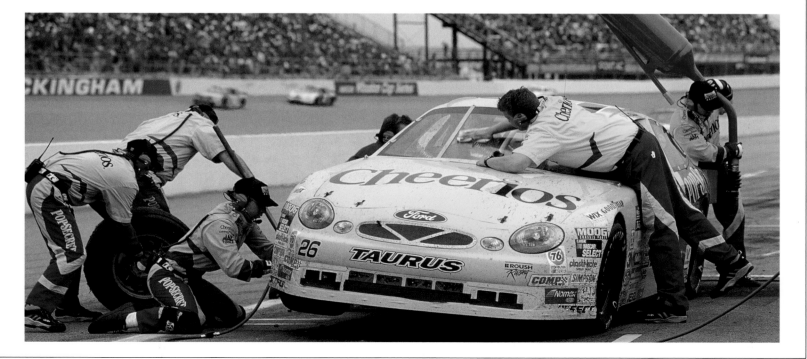

ULTIMATE STOCK CAR

2

THE CARS ARE the cornerstone of stock car racing. In no other form of racing does the vehicle share the spotlight with the athlete as it does in this one. Fans form allegiance with Fords and Chevys as easily as they do with drivers like Mark Martin and Jeff Gordon. Since day one of stock car racing, whether on a dusty oval cut from a Midwestern cornfield or a hard-packed rural Southern mountain road once trafficked by moonshiners, cars have been the stars. Almost anything that has been built in America has been tested in a stock car race. The 1951 Southern 500 at Darlington, South Carolina, saw 16 makes among the 59 entries. Why stock cars? "Win on Sunday, sell on Monday" was the motto. Bill France based the development of NASCAR on his firm belief that the average American would pay to see great drivers race family sedans on weekends, and he was right. The cars became the stars, and this is their story.

OUT OF THE DIRT

STOCK CARS WERE nowhere to be seen in the early days of American racing. Following the lead of the European circuits, much of the early American automobile racing was done in open-wheel cars. That slowly began to change in the late 1920s and early '30s, but the first nationally sanctioned racing series wasn't based in the Southeast. The American Automobile Association, forerunner of the United States Auto Club, began sanctioning races in the Midwest and the West during the years leading up to World War II. It wasn't until after the war, however, that stock car racing really took flight in the South. The early modifieds were dual-purpose cars that could also run moonshine when they weren't racing, and whiskey runners such as Roy Hall, Lloyd Seay, Bob Flock, Curtis Turner, Junior Johnson, and Gwyn Staley became legends when men and machines met on the dirt tracks each Saturday night. Many race promoters were even shadier than the drivers, however, which led Bill France to form NASCAR in 1947, giving stock car racing its first national organization.

◄ **THE FLYING FLOCKS**

Fonty Flock raced the 1952 Olds 88. The three Flock brothers were some of Oldsmobile's best customers. Between them, they scored 20 of Oldsmobile's first 39 NASCAR victories with Fonty winning 11 races for Olds to 7 for Tim and 3 for Bob.

Previous Spread
NARROW ESCAPE

Having crawled out the back window, Junior Johnson fled his still-rolling Pontiac as it came to a rest on the Beach-Road course at Daytona Beach, Florida, in 1956.

▼ **DUAL ROLE**

In the early years of stock car racing, one famous driver was Lloyd Seay, who had run whiskey out of the hills to the bootleg markets in Atlanta, Georgia.

1920-1950 The Dirt Foundation

SPEED AGE MAGAZINE COVER

MODERN RACES are held on high-speed asphalt ovals, but the sport's roots are firmly entrenched in dirt. Drivers today talk about how each track is different; in the days of dirt tracks, often each lap was different. Two-time NASCAR champion Herb Thomas recalled a track in Florida which was built only six inches above the water table. It looked good before the race began, but a few laps into the first heat, it was a muddy mess. On race day a track might be hard-packed and rutted, or slick and dusty. A 100-lap race on dirt could be run on a hundred different tracks because one that started muddy could finish dry and dusty.

▲ **LEFT IN THE DUST**

Riding out front like Fred Mahon did in his 1939 Ford was much easier than trying to drive through the dust clouds of a hot summer afternoon on a dry dirt oval.

◀ **FENDER BENDERS**

Frequent collisons battered the bodies of the cars, but seldom knocked them completely out of a race.

◀ **EARLY LEADER**

Fonty Flock's 1950 Oldsmobile took the lead of a 1950 race at Martinsville, Virginia, but Herb Thomas won the race in a rugged Hudson Hornet.

▼ RAISING DUST AT THE LAKE

Lakewood Speedway outside Atlanta, Georgia, was frequented by both moonshine drivers and professional racers. Lakewood hosted its first NASCAR race in 1951 with brothers and hometown favorites Tim and Bob Flock finishing 1-2, respectively.

▲ CRASH COURSE

Few dirt tracks had crash walls. At North Wilkesboro, North Carolina, a wooden fence marked the limits of the track.

▲ FLATHEADS RULE

The 1939 Ford coupe powered by Ford's flathead V8 engine was the car chosen by most Modified Division drivers running in the dirt.

▶ AT WORK IN THE DIRT

The Olds 88s of pole-sitter Wally Campbell (No. 18) and Tim Flock (No. 9) were prepared to lead the field into the 200-mile race on the one-mile dirt oval at Langhorne, Pennsylvania, on September 17, 1950.

1920-1950 Moonshining Hot Rods

EARLY STOCK CAR RACER

RUNNING MOONSHINE whiskey in the 1930s and '40s was a way of life in the South, and the best drivers became local folk heroes. Some of them, like Lloyd Seay and Roy Hall, never won a major sanctioned race. Others, like Curtis Turner, Junior Johnson, Bob Flock, and Gwyn Staley, went from the moonshine trade to being great racers. The preferred ride was anything with a big trunk like the '34 and '39 Fords, and the Caddies. The drivers were as ingenious as they were fast, mixing and matching engines to bodies to create the perfect car – one with a big engine and a huge trunk.

▲ **NIGHT RUNNING**
Black was a popular color for early stock cars because it was often used by whiskey runners, who did most of their work in the light of the moon.

◄ **HOT ROD LINCOLN**
Lincolns, like Tim Flock's, featured big trunks and V8 engines.

STOCK BEACH-ROAD RACER

◄ **CLANDESTINE CARGO**
The spacious trunk of the 1939 Ford Coupe could hold 64 quart bottles of contraband whiskey, making it the most popular delivery vehicle for the early moonshine racers.

▲ HOT COMPETITION
North Wilkesboro, North Carolina, was frequented by whiskey runners who wanted to try their hand at stock car racing.

▶ SOUPED-UP COUPE
One moonshiner who became a successful racer was Bob Flock, who drove the 1939 Ford coupe.

1920-1950 The 1939 Ford Flathead V8

1939 FORD COUPE

BEGINNING IN 1934, Ford built a series of coupes that became the staple of stock car racing and moonshine running for the next 15 years. These were the 1934, 1937, and 1939 models powered by the Ford flathead V8 engine. These engines could produce 90 hp and reach speeds of 110–115 mph on a good road. The chassis worked well on both the rutted dirt of early oval tracks and country roads. And the spacious trunk held up to 64 bottles of moonshine! Famed racer and moonshiner Lloyd Seay was once stopped for speeding near Atlanta. As the sheriff approached Seay's 1939 Ford, Lloyd calmly handed him two $10 bills. After the puzzled sheriff pointed out that the fine would be only $10, Seay smiled and said, "I know, but I'm payin' in advance since I will be coming back through here in a hurry later and won't be able to stop." The '34 and '39 Fords and their versatile drivers became part of racing folklore.

▲ **CONTROLLED CHAOS**

Drivers favored the 1934 (left) and '39 (other three cars) Fords because they were controllable while sliding through turns on either the open road or primitive Southern dirt tracks.

Side hood panel removed for cooling

Radiator recessed for protection

Extra holes cut in wheels to reduce weight

Stromberg carburetors

Racing gear shift handle

◀ **POWERED THE PIONEERS**

The Ford flathead V8 was continually modified over more than two decades as the primary short-track racing powerplant in the United States. This model featured three Stromberg carburetors.

▲ **PROVEN WINNER**

Owner Raymond Parks raced '39 Ford coupes for a decade. Fonty Flock won the 1947 Modified championship in a Parks-owned Ford.

FLATHEAD V8 FACTS

Ford produced three basic versions of its flathead V8. The original, called the "21 Stud," was produced in 1932. The 239-cubic-inch engine produced 90 hp. Upgraded two years later and now called the "24 Stud," it produced up to 110 hp. In 1939, Ford introduced the 254-cubic-inch version of the engine, which produced 115 to 120 hp. However, independent mechanics created a number of performance variations. Some 254s were bored out to 290 cubic inches with fancy heads and altered crankshafts. The modified engines produced up to 175 hp. Ford also produced a smaller 60-hp version that was designed for small panel delivery trucks. That engine soon found its way into open-wheel midget racers.

▲ HIGH-PROFILE RACER

The 1934 and 1936 Ford models' higher profile made them more prone to rolling over.

Red Vogt Special

Parks Novelty Machine Co.

14

Atlanta, Ga.

Running board

Large trunk favored by moonshiners

FRONT VIEW

SIDE VIEW

1920–1950 Big Bill and NASCAR

DRIVER BILL FRANCE

BILL FRANCE was moving his family to southern Florida in 1934 when he ran out of money in Daytona Beach and took a job painting houses. Within a year, he had resumed his racing career. But he saw his future as a race promoter, and after World War II he began staging races. On December 14, 1947, France and a group of promoters and racers founded the National Association for Stock Car Auto Racing, which would sponsor a racing series. To foster participation and loyalty to the series, France developed a points system that rewarded starting races as well as winning, with winners scoring no more than four times the points awarded for last place. Over the next half-century, NASCAR became the most powerful racing organization in the United States.

▲ **SPORTING GENTLEMEN**

Bill France Sr., the tall man in the back row, was a forceful figure at NASCAR's organizational meeting at the Streamline Hotel in Daytona Beach, Florida, in 1947.

◄ **RACING IN THE BLOOD**

Before he formed NASCAR, France also drove in races. His last appearance was in the 1950 Mexican Road Race, where he teamed with Curtis Turner.

▼ RACING ORGANIZES

For two seasons before the formation of NASCAR, Bill France ran the National Championship Stock Car Circuit with seven races in five states. His friends said the circuit wasn't big enough to be national, so France founded NASCAR on a larger scale.

Come In To
The Fastest Growing
Auto Racing Sport
In The U. S. A.

BILL FRANCE

RACE DATES AT
Greensboro, N. C.–June 15   North Wilkesboro, N. C.–June 22
Birmingham, Ala.–August 3
Greenville, S. C.   Columbia, S. C.
Daytona Beach, Fla.   Trenton, N. J.
ALSO AT SPARTANBURG, S. C., WITH JOE LITTLEJOHN
SEVERAL LOCALITIES YET TO BE LISTED

LINE UP
WITH BILL FRANCE
Operating as:
The National Championship Stock Car Circuit
"Leading the Nation in Stock Car Racing Promotions"

Write or Wire
BILL FRANCE
29 Goodall Avenue
DAYTONA BEACH, FLA.

▲ THE DRIVERS' FRIEND

A former racer himself, Bill France, seen here with Red Byron, had a close association with the drivers who ran in his events.

▲ TAKING IT ALL IN STRIDE

In the early days of the National Championship Stock Car Circuit, Bill France was omnipresent at races. He sold tickets, inspected the cars, ran the event, and helped clean up afterwards.

1950-1960

GAINING SPEED

MANY HAD COME to the new track on South Carolina's Darlington-Hartsville Highway just to see the experiment fail. A 500-mile stock car race? Cars of the era labored to finish 200-mile races. Now they would be running on asphalt on an oval more than a mile long. "The feeling was that either the distance or the speed would kill off the cars," Raymond Parks said. "I don't think anyone had much confidence because no one knew what was going to happen. The cars would be going twice as far as they had ever gone before at a higher speed. Everyone had questions. No one had an answer." Johnny Mantz did. The veteran of two Indy 500s equipped his Plymouth with modified truck tires. It was the slowest car in the field, but as rivals stopped time and again for new tires, Mantz – using a stopwatch to gauge speed – methodically clicked off laps, eventually winning by nine. That first Southern 500 set the standard, and races began moving from dirt tracks to paved ovals. By the end of the decade, cars were riding the high banks of Daytona International Speedway. In 1950, Mantz won the Southern 500 with an average speed of 76.26 mph. In 1959, Lee Petty won the first Daytona 500 with an average speed of 135.521 mph. Stock car racing was on the move.

◄ **PROGRESS**
Racing began to heat up in the 1950s as tracks like this one at Martinsville, Virginia, were paved with asphalt.

▼ **CIRCLING HISTORY**
Each race on the oval at Martinsville, Virginia, is a link to NASCAR's past. The circuit had been paved for more than 20 years when Dodges and Chevrolets battled in turn in 1978.

1950–1960 USAC

THE UNITED STATES Auto Club began sanctioning races in 1956 after the American Automobile Association withdrew from racing. For years USAC's stock car circuit was more national and diversified than NASCAR's and could match the southern circuit star for star. Richard Petty won a USAC race. So did Curtis Turner and Darrell Waltrip. USAC also allowed pony cars like the Camaro and Mustang to run alongside bigger sedans, using weight penalties to balance the difference in horsepower. But as NASCAR grew, the USAC stock car circuit shrank, and it was discontinued in 1984.

▲ **MR. VERSATILITY**

A. J. Foyt won three USAC championships and 41 races. In 1978–79, he drove a Camaro to back-to-back championships.

▲ **FLYING FURY**

Plymouth Furys, shown here, and Roadrunners carried driver Norm Nelson to 35 wins and two championships on the USAC stock car circuit.

ALL-TIME USAC STOCK CAR LEADERS

Season Championships

Driver	No.
1. Butch Hartman	5
2. A. J. Foyt	3
Dean Roper	3
Norm Nelson	3
5. Don White	2
Fred Lorenzen	2
Paul Goldsmith	2
Roger McCluskey	2

Career Race Wins

Driver	No.
1. Don White	53
2. A. J. Foyt	41
3. Norm Nelson	35
4. Butch Hartman	29
5. Paul Goldsmith	25
6. Roger McCluskey	23
7. Jack Bowsher	21

▲ MARIO GIVES CHASE

Don White's Dodge Charger leads
Mario Andretti's Ford during a 1967
USAC stock car race.

▲ DOMINATED AAA, TOO

Hudson Hornets dominated the AAA stock car series as well as the
NASCAR Grand National tour in the early 1950s. Hudsons won 43
USAC races over the four seasons.

▼ NORTH WILKESBORO, 1962

In the 1950s and 1960s, drivers often raced in both USAC
and NASCAR events. In this 1962 race at North Wilkesboro
Speedway, North Carolina, Ned Jarrett's Chevrolet (No. 11)
moved inside Jack Smith's Pontiac as the Fords driven by
Nelson Stacy (No. 29) and two-time USAC champion
Fred Lorenzen (No. 28) gave chase.

1950-1960 The Short Tracks

ON THE LAST day of September 1970, in Raleigh, North Carolina, Richard Petty won the Home State 200. It was the last Winston Cup race run on dirt. Only two tracks still on the Winston Cup schedule originally opened as dirt tracks. The track at Martinsville, Virginia, was paved in 1955 and the oval at Richmond, Virginia, in 1968. The switch from dirt to asphalt was not easy for some drivers, who were raised sliding through turns and battling the soft and muddy ruts of spring and the slick, sun-baked surfaces of summer. Richard Petty, David Pearson, and A. J. Foyt were equally at home on dirt and asphalt and they became superstars during the transition. But asphalt was easier on the maintenance teams, and once drivers and their crewmen mastered the art of tire selection and chassis setup, there would be no returning to dirt.

▲ **EVER-CHANGING TRACK**

A variety of cars sped along the rutted front straightaway at Martinsville, Virginia, where only a thin line of chalk separated the pit lane from the racing surface.

▼ **EARLY ASPHALT OVAL**

Martinsville, the only track on today's Winston Cup schedule that was also part of the 1949 schedule, was finally paved in 1955.

▶ **TRICKY INSIDE RAIL**

The third and fourth turns on the oval at North Wilkesboro, North Carolina, had an unusual feature. They were atop an incline and above the infield. Cars sliding to the inside of the track often went down an embankment.

BRISTOL

START/FINISH

The .533-mile oval at Bristol, Tennessee, is unusual because it didn't start out as a dirt track, like most other NASCAR short tracks. Bristol opened in 1961 as an asphalt oval with 36-degree banking in the turns and 16-degree banking on the short, 650-foot straightaways.

▲ DRAFTING

The concept of drafting – racing in long lines called trains – was one of the new tactics developed when racing shifted to asphalt tracks.

▶ TAKING IT TO THE BANK

Some dirt ovals featured the steep banking now a feature of superspeedways. It provided a second racing groove and allowed drivers to maintain higher speeds. It also improved drainage, so fewer races were canceled due to rain. The best-known such ovals were at Winchester and Salem, Indiana, and Marysville, Tennessee, and Dayton, Ohio (shown here).

1950-1960 The Fabulous Hudson Hornets

BEFORE 1948, the bodies of American passenger cars were placed on top of the frame rails. Running boards were needed to help passengers step into cars. Hudson Motor Company made history that year with its "step down" passenger compartment dropped between the rails. Hudson designed the car for passenger comfort, but Marshall Teague noticed that it improved road-hugging ability and saw its potential for NASCAR's new "strictly stock" class. Two years later, Hudson introduced its 308-cubic-inch L-head six and from 1951 to 1955, Hudsons won 143 races, including 79 on what is now NASCAR's Winston Cup circuit. They won three straight NASCAR season championships. Hudson was NASCAR's first factory team, and the factory produced option packages with upgraded shocks, wheels, rear axles, and manifolds to enhance its performance on the track.

▲ AN EARLY STAR

Dick Rathmann often had his name misspelled on his Hornet. He won 14 races and recorded 55 top-three finishes.

▼ HUDSON PIONEER

Marshall Teague won 22 races and two AAA titles for Hudson.

Flock said Hudsons "looked and acted like a football. When they flipped, they rolled and rolled."

◄ FIRST FACTORY TEAM

Herb Thomas (left) and Marshall Teague were drivers on stock car racing's first factory team.

Beefed-up wheels and hubs, shocks, and rear axle were part of the "export package."

Tim Flock won 10 races and the 1952 NASCAR Winston Cup championship for Hudson.

REAR VIEW

FRONT VIEW

Racing number

Solid chrome bumper

HUDSON HORNETS HIGHLIGHTS

From 1951–1955, Hudson Hornets competed on five major stock car series with astounding success. Hudson Hornets scored 143 wins, 112 seconds, and 72 thirds. Hudson's leading drivers:

	1st	2nd	3rd
Herb Thomas	43	24	11
Marshall Teague	22	10	5
Dick Rathmann	14	24	17
Tim Flock	10	7	4
Frank Mundy	9	4	6
Jim Reed	7	4	1
Lou Figaro	7	1	3
Danny Letner	6	1	1

Oversized radiator designed for racing

HERB THOMAS

LOUS HORNET HUDSON 92

▲ **92 WAS NO. 1**

Between 1951 and 1954, Herb Thomas amassed 38 victories, two NASCAR drivers' championships, and three car-owner titles driving the rugged Hudson Hornet.

Flat, slablike side panels.

1950-1960 Distinctive Cars

DRIVER BOB OLSON

ONE problem facing drivers, mechanics, and owners in the formative years of stock car racing was choosing the right car. There seemed to be as many answers as there were car models, and there were plenty to choose from. In NASCAR's first seven seasons, a dozen different brands made their way to Victory Lane. The preferred car for a dirt oval was heavy with a low center of gravity. As more tracks began to be paved, lighter cars that were easier on tires came into vogue. But for every diamond like the Olds 88, Hudson Hornet, and Chrysler 300 there were other cars that made an appearance on the tracks and quietly disappeared from the racing scene.

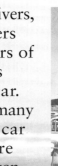

▲ LONG GONE

In 1950, NASCAR founder Bill France entered his final race as a driver, teaming with Curtis Turner in the Pan-American Road Race. Their choice for the long ride was the big and boxy Nash Ambassador.

▶ VARIETY OF MODELS

An Oldsmobile 88 (No. 41 ½) battled a Studebaker (No. 77) while a Lincoln (behind the Studebaker) and Dodge followed, and a Plymouth hugged the inside groove.

◀ WINNING THE GOLD

Arnold Smith drove a Studebaker Golden Hawk in races in the early '50s. Studebaker scored three NASCAR Winston Cup wins in 1951.

FIRST NASCAR WINSTON CUP WINS BY MAKE

Buick
Buck Baker, May 1, 1955, Charlotte Speedway, Charlotte, North Carolina.

Chevrolet
Fonty Flock, March 26, 1955, Columbia Speedway, Columbia, South Carolina.

Chrysler
Tommy Thompson, August 12, 1951, Michigan Fairgrounds, Detroit, Michigan.

Dodge
Lee Petty, February 1, 1953, Palm Beach Speedway, West Palm Beach, Florida.

Ford
Jim Florian, June 25, 1950, Dayton Speedway, Dayton, Ohio.

Hudson
Marshall Teague, February 11, 1951, Beach-Road course, Daytona Beach, Florida.

Jaguar
Al Keller, June 13, 1954, Linden Airport, Linden, New Jersey.

Lincoln
Jim Roper, June 19, 1949, Charlotte Speedway, Charlotte, North Carolina.

Mercury
Bill Blair, June 18, 1950, Vernon Fairgrounds, Vernon, New York.

Nash
Curtis Turner, April 1, 1951, Charlotte Speedway, Charlotte, North Carolina.

Oldsmobile
Red Byron, July 10, 1949, Beach-Road course, Daytona Beach, Florida.

Plymouth
Lee Petty, October 2, 1949, Heidelberg Speedway, Pittsburgh, Pennsylvania.

Pontiac
Marvin Panch, July 14, 1957, Memphis-Arkansas Speedway, Lehi, Arkansas.

Studebaker
Frank Mundy, June 16, 1951, Columbia Speedway, Columbia, South Carolina.

▲ CHRYSLER DOMINANCE

The team of white Chrysler 300s owned by Carl Kiekhaefer won 40 races in two years and swept the 1955 and 1956 NASCAR Winston Cup titles.

▼ FOREIGN AID

On June 13, 1954, NASCAR hosted its first road race on the airport runways at Linden, New Jersey. Paul Whiteman entered a Jaguar driven by Al Keller. It won the only victory ever by a foreign car in a NASCAR race.

Two-seat coupe

Standard split windshields

Split bumper drew protest

Sports car wheels and tires

1950-1960 Superspeedways

1960 DAYTONA RACING PROGRAM

THE IDEA OF a banked oval, which created a high-speed track with more than one groove, dates back to stock car racing's dirt foundation. NASCAR defines superspeedway as any oval over a mile in length, but Daytona and Talladega are most often associated with the term. Buddy Baker became the first driver in the world to break the 200-mph barrier on a closed course when he clocked a 200.477-mph lap at Talladega, Alabama, during a test of the Dodge Daytona on March 24, 1970. Twelve years later, Benny Parsons recorded the first 200-mph qualifying lap with a 200.176-mph clocking at Talladega in a 1982 Pontiac. Bill Elliott established both the Daytona (210.364 mph) and Talladega (212.809 mph) qualifying records in a 1987 Ford Thunderbird just before NASCAR moved to introduce restrictor plates to slow the cars.

▲ **AN EXCELLENT VIEW**

The tri-oval design and 24-degree banked turns of Texas Motor Speedway give everyone sitting in the grandstands a view of the entire 1.5-mile oval.

▼ **BIGGEST OF THE BIG**

The 2.66-mile, banked tri-oval track at Talladega Speedway in Alabama is NASCAR's longest and fastest racetrack..

◄ **COPYING INDY**

The field started three abreast for the first Southern 500 in 1950 at Darlington Raceway because 500-mile races at Indianapolis Motor Speedway are started that way.

◀ 400 LAPS

Opened a year after Daytona International Speedway in 1960, Lowe's Motor Speedway in Charlotte, North Carolina, is home to NASCAR's longest race – the annual Coca-Cola 600 on Memorial Day Weekend.

▼ PACK RACING

The combination of carburetor restrictor plate, a wide surface, and banked turns lead to extremely close "pack" racing at Daytona and Talladega.

LOWE'S MOTOR SPEEDWAY

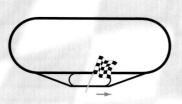

Lowe's Motor Speedway follows the proven design formula. The 1.5-mile oval has 24-degree banking in all four turns with a "tri-oval" turn at the start-finish line. Action on pit lane is easily seen from any seat in the main grandstands.

Darlington & the Southern 500

1950-1960

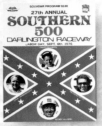

1976 PROGRAM

SOUTH CAROLINA'S famous Darlington Raceway remains one of NASCAR's cornerstone tracks a half-century after it was both the sanctioning body's first paved oval and first superspeedway. Harold Brasington got the idea of building it after visiting the Indianapolis Motor Speedway. The plot of land he coveted was owned by farmer Sherman Ramsey, who traded 70 acres for stock in the track – with one provision: Brasington couldn't touch a bait pond outside the first and second turns. This created a unique 1.25-mile oval with the first and second turns much tighter than the third and fourth turns, making it difficult to set up a car to get through both turns without a problem. Over time, the "Darlington stripe" became part of racing's vocabulary as cars scraped the walls in turns three and four. The first Southern 500 in 1950 was also NASCAR's first 500-mile race. Johnny Mantz, a midget racer with Indianapolis 500 experience, was the slowest qualifier but won by nine laps, driving slow to conserve his oversize tires while others stopped as frequently as once every ten laps.

▲ **MILLION-DOLLAR BILL**

Bill Elliott led the field into the first turn en route to winning the 1985 Southern 500. The victory gave Elliott the Winston Million for winning three of NASCAR's four major races.

▶ **EXPOSED PITS**

The original pits at Darlington were unprotected from the track. As workers toiled in the backstretch pits, cars were running at top speed only a few feet away.

DARLINGTON

START/FINISH

Darlington Raceway's unique pear shape is the result of the minnow pond that was originally outside the second turn. The track has been changed three times in its first half century. The original 1.25-mile oval is now 1.36 miles. The main straight was originally the old back straight. There is a 25-degree bank in the narrower first and second turns and 23 degrees in the sweeping third and fourth turns.

▼ THE DARLINGTON STRIPE

Richard Petty's ten-race winning streak in 1967 included a victory in the Southern 500. Though he dominated the race, Petty wasn't immune from getting a "Darlington stripe" on his right rear quarter panel.

▲ TWO BY TWO

Cars routinely run side by side at Darlington but seldom get three abreast on the straights due to the narrow track and tight entries to the corners. Jeff Gordon (No. 24), passing Geoff Bodine (No. 7) on the outside, won four straight Southern 500s (1995–1998).

▼ RUNNING STRONG AT 50

The Ford Taurus of pole-sitter Kenny Irwin is inside Ward Burton's Pontiac after taking the green flag to start the 50th Southern 500 on September 5, 1999.

1950-1960 The Olds 88

IN THE EARLY years of NASCAR, the battle for supremacy was between the Olds 88 and the Hudson Hornet. At the time Bill France launched NASCAR's Strictly Stock division in 1949, Oldsmobile had the perfect car – the two-door 88 series coupe powered by a 247-cubic-inch V8 engine. It was General Motors' high-performance car, and stood at the forefront of stock car racing until GM designated Pontiac as its racing model in 1960. The Olds 88 went from the hot rod of the late 1940s to the family car, but it won 85 races from 1949 to 1959 and carried Red Byron (1949), Bill Rexford (1950), and Lee Petty (1958) to NASCAR championships. The era was ending when Lee Petty won the inaugural Daytona 500 in an Oldsmobile in 1959.

▲ NASCAR's FIRST CHAMP

Red Byron won NASCAR's first Strictly Stock championship in 1949 with the V8-powered Olds 88. Oldsmobiles claimed 8 of the 11 races in the first season of what eventually became the Winston Cup Series.

◄ YIELDED TO HUDSON

The 1953 Olds won 9 races on the Grand National circuit and the 1954 design won 11 more.

Taped-over headlights to prevent breakage

▼ FAST ON THE SAND

Curtis Turner raced this Olds 88 on the Beach-Road course at Daytona Beach, Florida, on February 15, 1953. Bill Blair won the race in an Olds 88.

Extra wire mesh to protect radiator from rocks

▶ LEE PETTY'S OLDS

Lee Petty began racing Oldsmobiles in 1957 and won the NASCAR championship in 1958 with a Rocket 88. He switched back to Plymouths during the 1959 season, but not before winning the inaugural Daytona 500 driving an Oldsmobile.

OLDS 88 WIN LEADERS 1949–59	
Driver	Wins
1. Lee Petty	15
2. Fonty Flock	11
3. Curtis Turner	9
Buck Baker	9
5. Tim Flock	6
6. Junior Johnson	5
7. Herschel McGriff	4
Jim Paschal	4

▼ THE CHANGING 88

Tim Flock's 1954 Olds 88 won 11 of the season's 37 races. While Hudson kept the same design in the early 1950s, Oldsmobile made major changes while steadily upgrading the engine.

Stock windshield

Reinforced wheels for racing

Olds "Rocket 88" insignia

1950-1960 The Chrysler 300

*NASCAR PIONEER
CHARLIE SCOTT*

PUT THE MOST powerful cars in the hands of a perfectionist owner and the result is total domination. That was the case in 1955 and 1956 when Carl Kiekhaefer raced a stable of Chrysler 300s with hand-picked drivers. Chrysler had just introduced the 300-hp car and in only three months Kiekhaefer took control of stock car racing. In 1955, his drivers won both the NASCAR Grand National and AAA titles. A year later, his team won another NASCAR title. That season saw Kiekhaefer Chryslers winning 22 of 39 NASCAR races and 10 of 13 AAA events. Tim Flock won 18 of 39 races, a record that stood for 12 seasons. Kiekhaefer Chryslers won 22 races the next year also. Then, as quickly as he appeared, Kiekhaefer left racing, and Chrysler never won another title.

▲ FIRST CHECKERED FLAG

Tommy Thompson scored Chrysler's first NASCAR victory in Detroit, Michigan, on August 12, 1951.

▼ TOTAL DOMINATION

Before 1955, Chrysler had won a total of 9 NASCAR Winston Cup races, 7 by Lee Petty. Over the 1955–56 seasons, Chrysler won 50 of 91 races with the Carl Kiekhaefer team winning 44.

▼ 4 CARS, 1,380 HORSES

The Carl Kiekhaefer Chryslers at Daytona Beach, Florida, in 1956. From left: 300-C of Buck Baker, Dodge 500 of Speedy Thompson, 300-A of Tim Flock, and 300-B driven by Frank Mundy.

▲ END OF AN ERA

Buddy Arrington campaigned the last of the Chryslers in 1967.

CHRYSLER NASCAR WINNERS 1951–56

Driver	Wins
1. Tim Flock	21
2. Lee Petty	12
3. Buck Baker	9
4. Speedy Thompson	7
5. Fonty Flock	3
Herb Thomas	3
7. Tommy Thompson	1
Gober Sosebee	1
Norm Nelson	1

◄ POWER TO BURN

The Chrysler 300 was the first factory-built muscle car in America. The 1955 model was powered by a 331-cubic-inch, 300-hp engine. The 1956 version had 354 cubic inches and produced 340 hp – 55 more than its closest stock car rival. The Chrysler engine was distinctive because it had two carburetors.

▼ KIEKHAEFER AND FRIENDS

Carl Kiekhaefer with his drivers, from left, Herb Thomas, Buck Baker, and Speedy Thompson.

1950-1960 The Chevy Small-Block V8

CHEVROLET SAT on the sidelines as stock car racing took off in the early '50s. But with Ford showing interest in racing, Chevy replaced its aging Blue Flame Six engine with a small-block V8 in 1955. The 265-cubic-inch engine produced 225 hp and Chevy's first Winston Cup win at the 1955 Southern 500, but it was 1957 when the small block found its niche. Bored out to 283 cubic inches and fuel injected, the redesigned engine put out 1 hp per cubic inch. Quickly, NASCAR banned fuel injection, but Chevys won 21 of the Grand National tour's 53 races in 1957. Buck Baker won 10 and his second championship a year after driving the Chrysler 300 to the title. Although still officially on the sidelines, Chevrolet produced the *1957 Stock Car Competition Guide* to help customers transform the One-Fifty Utility Sedan into a NASCAR racer.

▲ SMALL-BLOCK COMPETITORS

The 1956 Chevrolets were underpowered when they competed in the 1956 Southern 500. Herb Thomas (No. 92) finished 49th and Gwyn Staley (No. 2) was 65th.

▲ OPEN AIR CHAMP

Bob Wellborn was the 1956 NASCAR Convertible Division champion racing this 1956 Chevrolet powered by the 265-cubic-inch small block engine.

▼ RACY RAGTOP

Bob Welborn won three straight NASCAR Convertible titles in Chevrolets. He repeated in the 1957 version of the model, which featured the 283-cubic-inch engine.

Convertible single roll bar

Standard wing windows

J.H. PETTY'S GARAGE
GREENSBORO, N.C.

Built By:
AUSTIN & RANDY
WELBORN

Car Donated By:
D.C. Saunders
In Memory of Iris

BOB WELBORN

49

Early NASCAR contingency sponsors

Exhaust pipe

Air cleaner

Distributor

Lifters and valves

Exhaust manifold

Starter

Piston

Fuel pump

Camshaft

Timing chain

2-barrel carburetor

Oil breather

Generator

Tarp to reduce turbulence

ED GADDY CHEVROLET
LENOIR, N.C.

GOODYEAR

▼ MIGHTY MIDGET

At a time when rivals added horsepower simply by adding cubic inches to the engine's displacement, Chevrolet created the refined small-block, 265-cubic-inch V8 in 1955. The original version produced 225 horsepower.

▼ LIGHTWEIGHT RACER

With less horsepower than the big-block V8s of Chrysler and other General Motors models, the Chevys weighed only 3,222 pounds, the lightest model in the Grand National Division.

61

1950-1960 The Pontiacs

PONTIAC'S SLIGHTLY WIDER front track provided an edge for the Bonnevilles of the early 1960s, but the breakthrough came by accident. Pontiac's new 389-cubic-inch V8 engine, which designers wanted positioned lower in the car, required the factory to push the wheels out so the exhaust headers would not hit the frame. Although it was less an engineering coup than the cheapest way out of a problem, the wider stance reduced wear on the right front tire. This change enhanced the Bonneville's capabilities as a race car, and Pontiacs went on to win 7 races in 1960, then 52 of 105 events in 1961 and 1962. Joe Weatherly won 20 races and the 1962 Winston Cup championship in a Pontiac.

▲ **GOOD-BYE TO THE BEACH**

Pontiacs won the last two races run on the fabled Beach-Road course. Cotton Owens (No. 6) scored Pontiac's first win in the 1957 beach race.

▲ **SEVEN-TIME WINNER**

Junior Johnson drove a Pontiac to seven wins in 1961, including three in August at Weaverville, North Carolina, and the Richmond and South Boston tracks in Virginia.

PONTIAC VICTORY MILESTONES	
1957	First win, Cotton Owens.
1960	10th win, Fireball Roberts.
1961	25th win, David Pearson.
1961	Pontiac drivers win 30 races.
1962	50th win, Jack Smith.
1963	Joe Weatherly wins 19 races in a season.
1991	100th win, Kyle Petty.

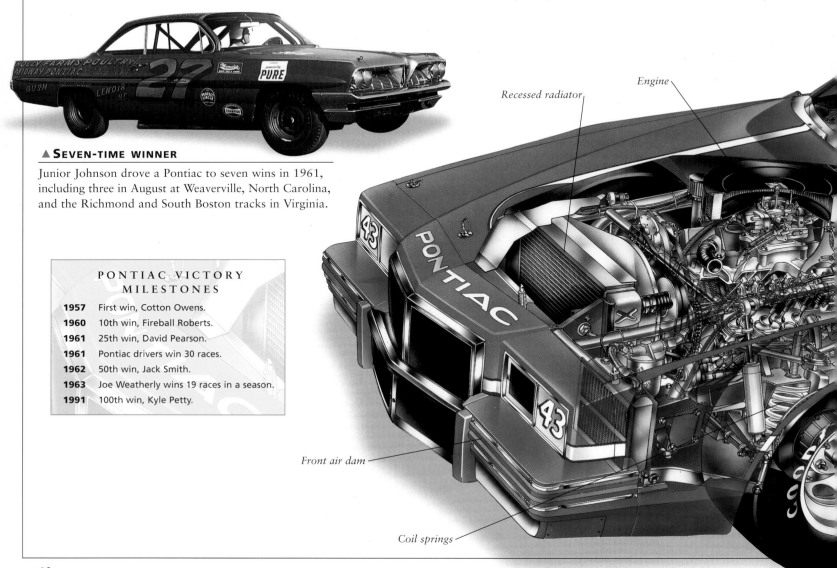

Recessed radiator

Engine

Front air dam

Coil springs

▼ SEASON OF STRUGGLE

Pontiac won 22 of the 53 races on NASCAR's premier circuit in 1962. Junior Johnson won his only race in the Bonneville at the National 400 at Charlotte Motor Speedway.

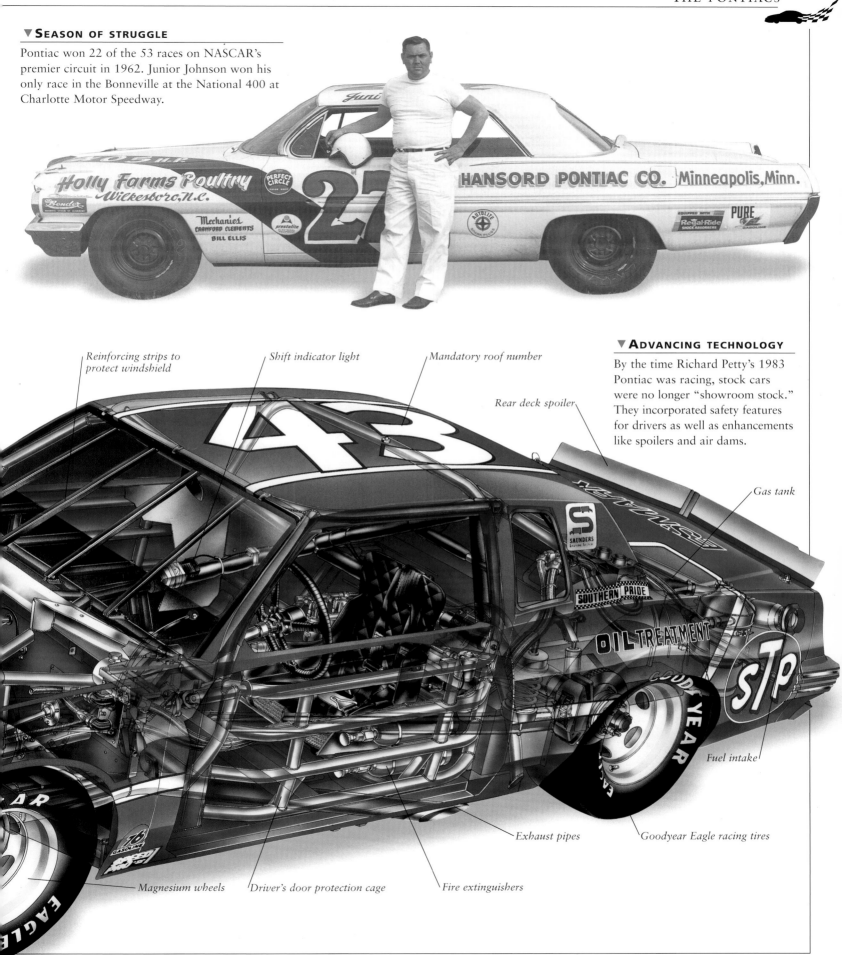

Reinforcing strips to protect windshield

Shift indicator light

Mandatory roof number

Rear deck spoiler

▼ ADVANCING TECHNOLOGY

By the time Richard Petty's 1983 Pontiac was racing, stock cars were no longer "showroom stock." They incorporated safety features for drivers as well as enhancements like spoilers and air dams.

Gas tank

Fuel intake

Goodyear Eagle racing tires

Exhaust pipes

Fire extinguishers

Driver's door protection cage

Magnesium wheels

1960-1965

REFINEMENTS

STOCK CAR RACING kicked into high gear in the early 1960s. A year after Florida's Daytona Motor Speedway opened, the superspeedways at Atlanta, Georgia, and Charlotte, North Carolina, debuted. The tour went west for a road race at Riverside, California, in 1963, and the new asphalt speedways at Bristol, Tennessee, and Rockingham, North Carolina, also came on line. New tracks were faster and so were the new cars. Car builders no longer needed compromise designs that could race on ruts as well as high-banked asphalt tracks. Engines grew as cars got lower, wider, and lighter. Speeds jumped perceptibly. The qualifying speed for the inaugural Daytona 500 in 1959 was 143.198 mph – which, at the time, was almost 35 mph above the next fastest track. Five years later speeds at Daytona had reached 175 mph. Emphasis was on speed, but the gains came with a price. Safety measures lagged behind and good men died. This triggered a series of safety gains that remain the cornerstone of stock car racing to this day – the fire suit, tire interliner, full cage, safety helmet, and in-car radios.

◄ **SAFETY CAGE**

A series of accidents involving the driver's side door inspired veteran car builder Cotton Owens to design a new roll cage with bars in the door. Studying the new concept with Owens was driver David Pearson.

▼ **PIT DANCE**

The Wood brothers choreographed their pit stops, changing the way cars pitted for gas and tires – and revolutionizing the tactics of stock car racing.

1960-1965 Speed with Safety

EARLY DRIVER'S APPAREL

LEE PETTY WAS the patriarch of a four-generation family in stock car racing. But the first three-time Winston Cup champion's biggest contribution to the sport might have been his promotion of safety. He studied everything from roll cages to padded steering wheels to side window screens. Safety didn't become a major issue until the early 1960s, when the potent combination of more powerful cars racing on bigger, faster superspeedways resulted in several horrific accidents. Officials were forced to take a close look at safety. Today, tubular frames, fire suits, advanced helmets, fuel cells, and tire interliners are standard equipment. All were developed in the 1960s.

▲ DRIVER PROTECTION

Many safety features on the modern stock car can be traced to the early 1960s and the rise in speeds brought on by superspeedways. The driver's compartment of Steve Park's Chevrolet Monte Carlo doubles as a safety cell.

▶ REDUCED FIRE RISK

After several fatal racing fires, the Firestone Tire & Rubber Company developed the fuel cell, which suspends fuel in fireproof foam.

▼ REDUCED FIRE RISK

In the pits, gas men now wear helmets for protection.

Protected engine compartment

Specially engineered Goodyear tires

Reinforced firewall

1950　　　　　　1955　　　　　　1965

1970　　　　　　1990　　　　　　2000

▲ HEAD PROTECTION

Early racing helmets were little more than construction hardhats. Earflaps were added during the 1950s and most drivers went to football-style helmets by the mid-1960s. By the 1990s, the development of lightweight composites led to the development of the modern helmet.

▲ NO BLOWOUT

One fear of drivers – tire blowouts – diminished in 1965 with the development of the interliner – a tire within the tire. With the outer tire punctured, the car could ride back to the pits on the interliner.

◄ THE PROTECTIVE SKELETON

The driver's defense in an accident is a maze of steel and chrome-moly tubing welded into a protective frame. The design begins with the roll cage and extends to the bumpers. The body is hung on the frame.

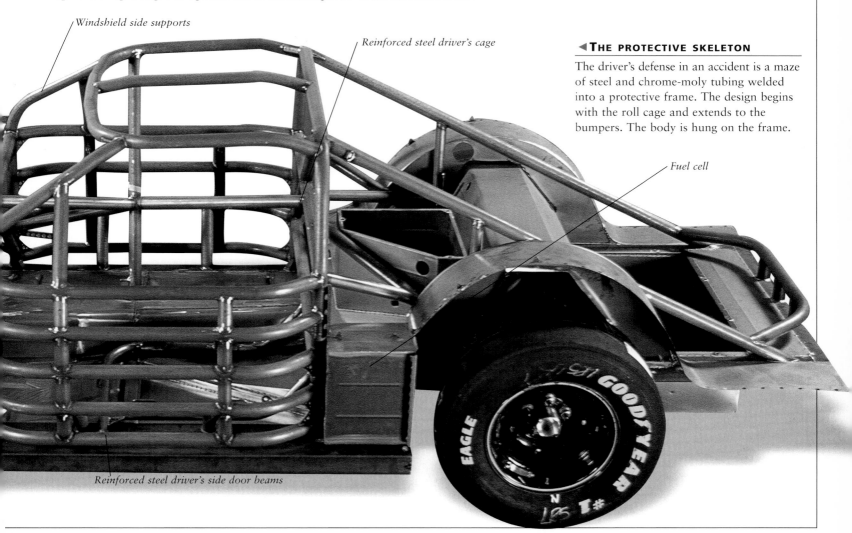

Windshield side supports

Reinforced steel driver's cage

Fuel cell

Reinforced steel driver's side door beams

1960-1965 Drag Racing

CAMARO DRAG RACER

AFTER THE SECOND World War, many returning soldiers began building customized cars, matching the best available bodies and most powerful V8 engines they could find. Most of the bodies predated the war. These small coupes – Willys, Ford, Crosley, American Austin, Studebaker, Fiat, Oldsmobile, and Nash Metropolitan – were paired with altered V8 engines. The hot rod was born. Soon enthusiasts were staging clandestine drag racing meets across the nation. Wally Parks, who helped launch *Hot Rod* magazine in 1947, formed the National Hot Rod Association (NHRA) in 1951. Sanctioned by the NHRA and the International Hot Rod Association (IHRA), drag races matching every form of car imaginable sprang up on quarter-mile strips in every corner of the nation. The "gas coupes" division led to the "altered" and "stock" classes that are the foundation of drag racing today.

▲ MODIFIED BASICS

This 1955 Chevrolet featured racing slicks in the back with a smaller-than-stock front wheel assembly.

▼ VARIETY

A blown Chevrolet Corvette (right) faced a modified Austin Healey at Kentucky's Bluegrass Raceway.

Roll bar

Braking parachute

Blower air intake

Racing slicks

Exhaust pipe

▲ HORSEPOWER RULES

The Ford 426-cubic-inch engine made a potent drag racing machine of this fastback Ford.

▲ CYCLONE

The American muscle car found a home in drag racing. Rob Guilford's Mercury Cyclone competed in stock-based classes in the 1970s.

◄ TRIPPING THE LIGHTS

A Camaro jumped off the line during the NHRA 1971 Winternationals in Pomona, California.

High front suspension for weight transfer

1960-1965 The Petty Legacy

RICHARD PETTY

BILL FRANCE created NASCAR, but the Petty family from Level Cross, North Carolina, put stock car racing on the map. Lee drove in NASCAR's first Strictly Stock race in 1949, was the first three-time national champion, and ranks seventh on the career victory list with 55 wins. In 1960, Lee was the first NASCAR driver to reach the 50-win milestone. That year his son, Richard, won his first race. Before he was finished in 1992, Richard had started 1,177 races, won 200, and been crowned champion seven times. Richard was NASCAR's first superstar. His son, Kyle, carried the tradition forward. And on April 2, 2000, 19-year-old Adam, Kyle's son, was the first fourth-generation driver to start a Winston Cup race. Three days after Adam's debut, however, Lee passed away at the age of 86. And on May 12, Adam died in an accident while practicing for a race at London, New Hampshire. Between them, the Pettys started over 2,200 races and won 263 of them.

▲ **FOUR GENERATIONS**

From left, Lee, Richard, Kyle, and Adam Petty, racing's most famous family, gathered around the Petty Enterprises transporter.

Factory emblem

▲ **P – FOR PETTY, PLYMOUTHS**

Richard Petty stood with his 1963 Plymouth that won 14 races. Plymouths took Lee and Richard to 156 wins.

Air dam

◄ SETTING THE BAR

Lee Petty (No. 42), NASCAR's first three-time champion, was also the first driver to win 50 races in his career.

► CHIP OFF THE BLOCK

Kyle Petty won the first race he ever entered. Three of his eight career wins came at Rockingham, North Carolina.

▲ FOLLOWING DAD

Richard Petty won the 1964 Daytona 500. His first Daytona victory came five years after father Lee won the inaugural Daytona 500.

▼ PROMISE UNFULFILLED

Adam Petty was 18 when he started racing a Chevrolet Monte Carlo on the NASCAR Busch Grand National Series in 1999. He had three top-five finishes.

PETTY RACING HIGHLIGHTS

1949 Lee Petty's first win (also first win for Plymouth).

1954 Lee Petty wins first championship.

1959 Lee Petty wins first Daytona 500 in a photo finish.

1960 Richard Petty wins first Winston Cup race.

1960 Lee Petty wins 55th and last race.

1964 Richard Petty wins first of record seven Daytona 500s.

1964 Richard Petty wins first NASCAR Winston Cup title.

1967 Richard Petty wins 56th race to pass father as NASCAR's all-time Winston Cup leader.

1967 Richard Petty sets NASCAR records with 27 wins in a season and 10 straight wins.

1969 Richard Petty wins 100th race.

1979 Kyle Petty starts first Winston Cup race.

1984 Richard Petty wins 200th race.

1986 Kyle Petty wins first Winston Cup race.

1992 Richard Petty makes last Winston Cup start.

2000 Adam Petty makes first Winston Cup start.

Radio antenna

Roof rail

Rear spoiler

Exhaust pipes

Junior Johnson's Chevys

GENERAL MOTORS ENDED its factory program with Pontiac in 1963. As GM quit, it sold a batch of its 427-cubic-inch V8 engines and crates of parts to car owners Ray Fox and Junior Johnson. The year also witnessed a major offensive by Ford and Chrysler. Johnson's strategy then was "go or blow." He won nine poles and seven races and dropped out of 20. He led almost every race he started. Ford cried foul. Surely he must be cheating. Said Junior: "They haven't caught me if I am." And he smiled – all year long.

JUNIOR JOHNSON

▲ A LANDSLIDE VICTORY

With NASCAR official John Bruner Jr. looking on, Junior Johnson took the checkered flag with no one else in sight at Orange Speedway in Hillsborough, North Carolina, on March 10, 1963.

◄ FIRM GRIP ON FIRST

Junior Johnson's first win of 1963 in his renegade Chevy was in a Daytona 500 qualifying race at Daytona International Speedway.

▼ THE CHICKEN CARS

Rex Lovette, president of Holly Farms, came into racing as Junior Johnson's sponsor in 1963, one of the first nonautomotive sponsors in NASCAR Winston Cup racing.

▲ MOVE OVER, FIREBALL

Junior Johnson powered under Fireball Roberts to take the lead of the 1963 Daytona 500. Johnson later blew his engine while leading.

JUNIOR JOHNSON HIGHLIGHTS

Junior Johnson started 32 races in 1963 with the one-of-a-kind Chevrolet he referred to as his "Mystery Car." He won nine poles and started 16 races from the front row. Johnson's Chevy won seven races, including the Dixie 400 at Atlanta Motor Speedway and the National 400 at Charlotte Motor Speedway. It also placed second twice and third twice for a total of 11 top-three finishes. The Chevy dropped out of the other 21 races it started. Like Johnson said of the car, "We go until we blow."

1960-1965 ARCA and ASA

THE AUTOMOBILE RACING Club of America (ARCA) was the Midwest Auto Racing Club when it was organized in 1953 by John Marcum, a friend of Bill France Sr. ARCA uses engine (358-cubic-inch V8) and body styles similar to the Winston Cup series, but the series stretches from superspeedways to dirt tracks. The American Speed Association (ASA) was formed in 1967. It also uses Ford Taurus, Chevy Monte Carlo, and Pontiac Grand Prix bodies, but engine specs were changed from a 275-cubic-inch V6 in 1999 to the unique, fuel-injected Vortec V8 developed by GM for ASA. ASA has been a training ground for drivers like Mark Martin, Rusty Wallace, and Alan Kulwicki.

▲ MARTIN CLOSES IN

Mark Martin (No. 2) is the only driver to win three consecutive ASA titles (1978–80). He won a fourth in 1986, and a total of 22 ASA races. In this 1980 race on the half-mile oval at Mt. Clemens, Michigan, Martin gave chase to Rusty Wallace (No. 66) and Harold Fair (No. 81).

◄ FLYING FORD

Jack Bowsher won three straight ARCA titles from 1963 to 1965 driving a Ford. He ranks second all-time in career ARCA wins with 48.

Windshield support bar

Hood safety latches

Airbrushed headlights

▲ TURF WARS

Rusty Wallace became the tenth driver to win 50 NASCAR Winston Cup races in 2000. But 20 years earlier, Wallace battled to keep pace with ASA king Bob Senneker (No. 84).

◄ BEFORE THE JUMP

Benny Parsons drove his Ford Torino to back-to-back ARCA championships in 1968–69 before advancing to the NASCAR circuit. He was the Winston Cup champion in 1973.

▼ SENNEKER RULES

Bob Senneker won only one season championship, in 1990, but he is the ASA's all-time leader with 85 race wins.

Rear spoiler

Large fuel intake for easy refueling

Driver cooling vent

Centering hub

1960-1965 The Pit Stop

BY TODAY'S STANDARDS, a 20-second pit stop for four tires and a tank of gas is ordinary. But in the 1950s, even the best pit stops often lasted over a minute. "We didn't think about the time in the pits," said veteran mechanic Junie Donlavey. "We changed tires with a four-prong lug wrench and poured gas through a funnel." The Wood brothers changed all that in the early 1960s. With choreographed strategy and new three-pump jacks and fuel cans, they quartered the time it took to make a pit stop. Suddenly, races were won and lost in the pits. The sign calling for the Wood Brothers' No. 21 to pit raised as much anticipation among fans as a pass on the track.

WOOD BROTHERS PIT CREWMAN

▲ A BREAK FROM THE RACE

Early pit stops were not known for their furious action. As owner Joe Littlejohn discussed strategy with driver Curtis Turner, Frank Christian poured a five-gallon can of gas into the Oldsmobile through a funnel.

▼ NO WASTED MOTION

The Wood Brothers pit crew sprang into action on David Pearson's Mercury with each man knowing his task and the time allotted for it.

Gasman with 11-gallon cans

▲ FIVE-MAN JOB

Before the Wood brothers' innovations, the pit scene often included a helpless onlooker or two.

▲ POETRY IN MOTION

Every member of the Wood Brothers crew was assigned specific tasks set against the clicking of a stopwatch. Leonard Wood was the crew's right front tire changer.

▲ THE JUNKYARD DOGS

That is how Dale Earnhardt's crew came to be known. David Smith hoisted one of the new single-pump aluminum-titanium jacks while Will Lind made a chassis adjustment.

Tire carrier

Rear tire changer

Jackman

Front tire changer

1960-1965

Officials: Keeping It Real

FLAGMAN JOHN BRUNER

LEFT UNCHECKED, the men who build stock cars can create wonderful machines. But they wouldn't be stock, and the driver with the most innovations would probably win most of the time. There have to be rules for car builders and drivers as well as for promoters. To enforce the rules, NASCAR maintains a corps of officials to inspect everything from the size and shape of an engine's cylinders to the capacity of the cars' fuel tanks. The officials hope to stay one step ahead of car builders, who are constantly looking for loopholes, and more than eager to leap through any they find.

▲ **EVEN ON THE BEACH**
Technical inspectors examined the engine of a Chevrolet convertible before a race on Daytona Beach, Florida's Beach-Road course.

◄ **AND HE MEANS IT**
Jimmy Cox is the NASCAR official in charge of the pit lane exit at Winston Cup races. Cox makes sure cars don't jump the pace car during cautions and blend in at the back of the pack. Running his stop sign could cost a driver a lap and a shot at victory.

Front air dam

Headlight decals

▼ CHECKED THOROUGHLY

Each car is inspected up to three times before a NASCAR Winston Cup race. A roof template ensures that the top lines of each car conform precisely to guidelines.

▲ BEFORE

NASCAR officials used a common template to measure the roof of the Morgan-McClure Chevrolet before a 1993 race.

▲ AFTER

The Morgan-McClure Chevy no longer fit the templates after driver Ernie Irvan's brush with the outside wall. A NASCAR official awaited the car's removal from pit road.

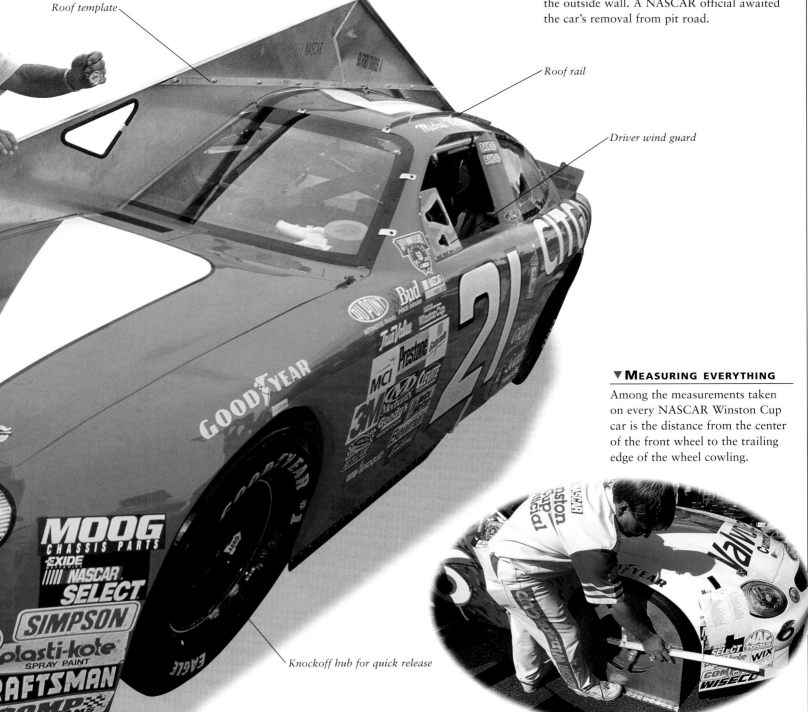

Roof template

Roof rail

Driver wind guard

▼ MEASURING EVERYTHING

Among the measurements taken on every NASCAR Winston Cup car is the distance from the center of the front wheel to the trailing edge of the wheel cowling.

Knockoff hub for quick release

1960-1965 The Chrysler Hemi

THE IDEA OF hemispherical heads on engines to increase air flow to the carburetors was not born at Chrysler in the 1960s. Cotton Owens saw it in World War II and used hemis during the early '50s. The Carl Kiekhaefer Chryslers of 1955 and 1956 were hemis, but they left racing before NASCAR could change the rules. Chrysler returned to racing in 1963 with the hemi. The result was high speed, new rules, and a boycott. Dodges and Plymouths won 26 races in 1964, and a Plymouth broke the Daytona 500 qualifying record by nearly 10 mph. NASCAR penalized Chrysler teams with weight requirements, and they withdrew. When they returned in 1965, hemis could only race on superspeedways in heavier Plymouth Fury and Dodge Polara models. By 1967, the hemi was gone from NASCAR.

▲ A FRENCH DESIGN

The hemi engine of the French V8 Darracq of 1906 produced 200 hp and a top speed of 122.449 mph.

▲ POWERING PETTY

Richard Petty won the first of his seven NASCAR Winston Cup titles in 1964 behind the wheel of a Plymouth Belvedere powered by a hemi engine. Petty won nine races and eight poles during the season.

▶ AMERICAN MUSCLE

Simply called the "Cuda," the 1969 Plymouth Barracuda was the ultimate in American muscle cars of the era. Its power-to-weight ratio made it a popular drag racer as well as a street machine. Vintage Barracudas are still raced today in sanctioned drag meets.

Carburetor air intake

Fog lamp

Hood safety latches

◀ **TIGHT SQUEEZE**

The 429-cubic-inch Chrysler V8 hemi engine left little room for anything else when packed into the engine compartment of the Plymouth Barracuda.

▶ **BIG BURNER**

The Chrysler hemi engine which was first manufactured in the 1960s is still the basis of the powerplant for many of drag racing's Top Fuel Dragsters.

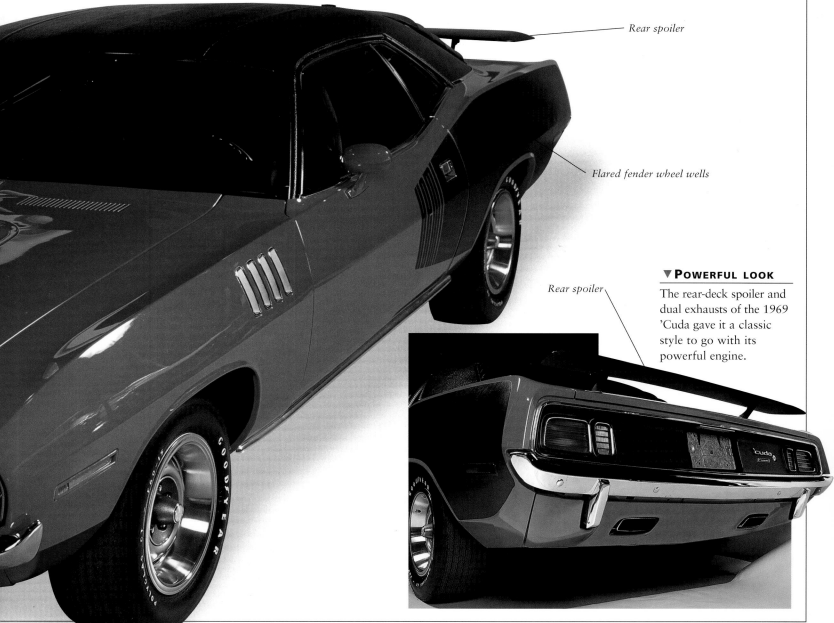

Rear spoiler

Flared fender wheel wells

Rear spoiler

▼ **POWERFUL LOOK**

The rear-deck spoiler and dual exhausts of the 1969 'Cuda gave it a classic style to go with its powerful engine.

1965-1975

FIERCE COMPETITION

STOCK CAR RACING rode point as all of motor racing soared to new heights in the mid-1960s. New stars replaced NASCAR's pioneers. The Richard Petty-David Pearson rivalry grabbed national headlines and Cale Yarborough, Bobby Isaac, Bobby Allison, and Buck Baker joined the cast. IndyCar stars A. J. Foyt and Mario Andretti won the Daytona 500, Andretti in 1967, Foyt in 1972. Stock car drivers Bobby and Donnie Allison, Cale Yarborough, and LeeRoy Yarbrough raced in the Indy 500. The Wood brothers went to Indianapolis, revolutionizing pit stops in open-wheel racing as they had in stock cars. A new type of stock car racing arrived with the Ford Mustang and the American "pony" car. The Trans-American Series began in 1966 as a road racing tour for smaller sports sedans. Factories quickly became involved, which attracted drivers like Mark Donohue, Parnelli Jones, George Follmer, and Peter Revson to a tour that briefly competed with NASCAR for popularity. The American sports fan, however, loves a rivalry, and nothing could match Petty vs. Pearson.

◄ **RIVALS**

Richard Petty and David Pearson finished 1-2 a total of 63 times in their careers, with Pearson enjoying a 32-31 edge on "The King" in their showdowns.

▼ **ROUSH RULES**

Before forming his own NASCAR Winston Cup team, Jack Roush built Ford Mustangs for road racing. His Mustangs won nine straight GTO titles in the 24 Hours of Daytona.

1965-1975   TRANS-AM

DAN GURNEY

THE EMERGENCE of Ford's Mustang in 1964 changed the landscape of the American car industry. Although not a pure sports car, the light, powerful, and relatively inexpensive Mustang reached a younger, performance-minded market. The Mustang's popularity triggered development of a number of copycats, including the Mercury Cougar, Chevy Camaro, Pontiac Firebird, AMC Javelin, and Plymouth Barracuda. Each design was sportier and more powerful than the last. To boost sales, factories became involved in racing, and they chose the road-racing Trans-Am circuit formed in 1966 by the Sports Car Club of America. The series' success led to the ill-fated NASCAR Grand-Am Division as well as the IMSA GTP, GTO, and GTU classes.

▲ PLENTY OF HORSES

The prototype Trans-Am pony car was the Ford Mustang. Parnelli Jones drove a Mustang to seven wins and the 1970 series championship.

◀ FACTORY HOPES

Struggling AMC hoped success for its Javelin would drive sales. Driven by Mark Donohue, this Javelin won the 1971 Trans-Am title after finishing second in its 1970 debut.

▲ DODGE'S CHALLENGER

Chrysler entered the Trans-Am fray with a two-pronged effort in 1970 with Sam Posey in the Challenger.

▼ FLYING FISH

Plymouth campaigned two Barracudas in the first Trans-Am Series of 1966, but raced a limited schedule after that. This one was driven by Dan Gurney.

TOP TRANS-AM WINNERS	
Chevrolet Camaro	8
Ford Mustang	7
Chevrolet Corvette	5
AMC Javelin	2
Mercury Capri	2
Porsche Carrera	2
Porsche 934	2
Jaguar XJS	2
Alfa Romeo GTA	2

▼ TRIAL BY RACE

The strength of the early Trans-Am Series was the factory competition. This 1969 race featured Ford Mustangs and Chevrolet Camaros, plus a Pontiac Firebird, an AMC Javelin, and a Dodge Challenger.

Mustangs & Mercury Cougars

1965-1975

TINY LUND

WITH TRANS-AM racing challenging NASCAR's Winston Cup Series for national media attention in the late 1960s and early 1970s, Ford diverted considerable resources to both the Trans-Am and NASCAR Grand American circuits. Carroll Shelby, Bud Moore Engineering, and Holman-Moody all were involved with the "pony car" circuits. Ford's Trans-Am programs also attracted top drivers such as Dan Gurney, Parnelli Jones, Peter Revson, George Follmer, and Peter Gregg. In the Grand-Am Series, brothers Bobby and Donnie Allison and Tiny Lund carried the Ford hopes. However, after Jones won five races to claim Mustang's second title in four years in 1970, Ford's interest in the Trans-Am Series waned. It wasn't until Jack Roush returned with a factory-backed program in the mid-1980s that Ford resumed racing in the Trans-Am and IMSA GTO series.

▲ COUGARS CRUSADE

The Mercury Cougars dominated NASCAR's Grand-Am series in 1968. Tiny Lund (No. 15) led teammate Bud Moore and the Mustang of Donnie Allison.

▼ FASTBACK

The fastback Mustang debuted on both the Trans-Am and Grand-Am circuits in 1968.

▲ DESIGN CHANGES

The Mustang that Ford introduced to racing was much like the street version of the original two-door coupe.

Headlight covers

Air dam

▲ **AT THE LIMIT**

The original Trans-Am rules called for a V8 maximum engine size of 305 cubic inches. Bobby Allison's fastback Mustang was near the maximum at 302 cubic inches.

Driver's shoulder belt

▲ **FIRST TRANS-AM FORD**

Ford moved quickly into Trans-Am racing, hiring Bud Moore (left) to head a factory operation. The first entry was a Mercury Cougar driven by Parnelli Jones (next to Moore).

Exhaust pipe

Chevy Camaro/Pontiac Firebird

PONTIAC FIREBIRD

EVEN BEFORE FORD had formally introduced the Mustang, General Motors was designing its own "pony car" sports coupe. Just as quickly as the Chevrolet Camaro and Pontiac Firebirds rolled into production, they were challenging the Dodge Darts, Ford Mustangs, and Plymouth Barracudas on the Trans-Am road racing series. Originally powered by 303-cubic-inch V8s, the Camaros and Firebirds proved excellent racing designs and their applications quickly spread beyond Trans-Am. Although Camaros won 25 Trans-Am races in less than five years as well as a NASCAR Grand-Am championship, Chevrolet ended its Trans-Am program in favor of becoming the single car used in the International Race of Champions (IROC) series from 1975 to 1989. Corvettes won four Trans-Am titles between 1975 and 1981 when General Motors returned both its Firebird (now called the Firebird Trans-Am) and Camaro lines to Trans-Am. In the next dozen years, Firebird Trans-Ams and Camaros won seven championships.

▲ **DIRT TRACKING**

Tiny Lund's Camaro led Jim Paschal during one of the oval dirt races that were part of NASCAR's 1969 Grand American Series.

▼ **TOO MUCH FUN**

Buck Baker had retired from stock car racing when he returned to drive the Pontiac Firebird in NASCAR's short-lived Grand American Series.

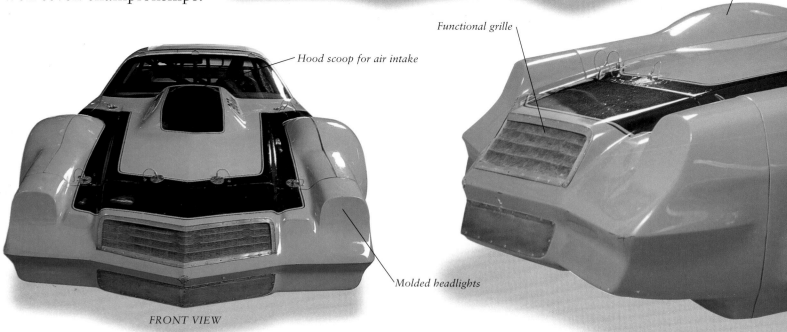

Molded flared fenders

Functional grille

Hood scoop for air intake

Molded headlights

FRONT VIEW

▶ Quick chevy

Chevrolet countered Ford's entry into Trans-Am with Z-28 Camaros prepared by Roger Penske. Here, Sam Posey drove one of Penske's famed Sunoco Camaros powered by a 450-hp Traveco Chevy V8.

◀ Dual winner

The 1969 Camaro, here driven by Tiny Lund, won titles in both the Trans-Am and NASCAR's rival Grand American Series.

Side mesh protector

Rear spoiler

▲ Modified camaro

Richie Evans was known as NASCAR's King of Modifieds. He was also an expert at building short-track cars like this Camaro. Evans won nine NASCAR Modified season championships, four NASCAR Northeast Region titles, and more than 500 short-track races.

The Holman-Moody Galaxie

IN 1957 THE Automobile Manufacturers Association withdrew their factories from racing. The move caught Ford's powerful racing operation by surprise. Ford hadn't been involved in racing prior to 1955, but in two short years they had become the dominant force in stock car racing. Fords had won 27 NASCAR races in 1956 and 15 of the first 21 races in 1957 when the decision came. Out of the ashes rose one of the most powerful teams in racing. John Holman and Ralph Moody formed a partnership that bought all of Ford's racing stock and launched one of racing's first research and development programs. Between 1957 and 1971, almost every Ford that reached the winner's circle had a Holman-Moody connection, and their influence extended beyond stock car racing. Their shops produced cars that won the 24 Hours of Le Mans. The Holman-Moody name became synonymous with speed among drivers, owners, and fans.

▲ **PARTS OF THE PROGRAM**

Ned Jarrett won the 1965 NASCAR championship in a Ford owned by Bondy Long. But the parts originated with Holman-Moody.

▲ **THE HORSEPOWER TWINS**

Ralph Moody (left) and John Holman brought special talents to the job. Moody was an expert in mechanics and driver training while Holman was a genius in organization and development.

▼ THE EXTENDED FAMILY

Standing alongside his Galaxie, Nelson Stacy was one of the drivers who raced Holman-Moody Fords in the 1960s.

▼ FIREBALL ROBERTS

One of Holman-Moody's favorite drivers was Fireball Roberts, who won the 1963 Southern 500 in a Holman-Moody Galaxie.

◄ COVERING THE FIELD

For more than a decade, almost every Ford in every NASCAR race had a connection to the Holman-Moody team. Holman-Moody driver Fred Lorenzen ran inside Joe Weatherly during the 1960 Daytona 500.

1965-1975

The Exotic Superbirds

*BUDDY BAKER'S
1971 DODGE CHARGER*

NASCAR HAS never claimed to be ahead of the curve in terms of technology. To this day, Winston Cup cars have carbureted engines with rear-wheel drive while most passenger cars are fuel-injected with front-wheel drive. But during 1969 and 1970, NASCAR featured two truly futuristic models: the high-winged Dodge Daytona and the Plymouth Superbird. Both cars were aerodynamic makeovers of the Dodge Charger 500; the changes were a pointed nose and semi-fastback rear deck that supported a spoiler. A Dodge Daytona set a closed-course stock car speed record of 201.104 mph on November 24, 1970, at Talladega Speedway in Alabama. The record stood until 1983. Alas, the Daytonas and Superbirds did not last as long. In 1971 NASCAR reduced their engine size from 426 to 305 cubic inches.

▲ THE FLYING WING

The rear wing of the Plymouth Superbird was 25 inches above the rear deck. Rival drivers claimed the wings limited their forward vision and created turbulence.

Brake air vents

Pointed nose

▲ PETTY SWITCHED

After driving a Ford through most of the 1969 season, Richard Petty went back to Plymouth in 1970 and won 18 races, the third-highest season total of his career.

▲ WINGED WARRIORS

Nearly identical Dodge Daytonas driven by Charlie Glotzbach and Bobby Allison battled during the 1970 Daytona 500.

High-wing air spoiler

Semi-fastback rear deck

▲ THE BARRIER BREAKER

On March 24, 1970, at Alabama's Talladega Superspeedway, Buddy Baker became the first driver to record a 200-mph lap on a closed course in this Dodge Daytona.

David Pearson's Mercurys

1965-1975

DAVID PEARSON AFTER VICTORY

THE BIGGEST winners on the Winston Cup circuit in the early 1970s were the Plymouths and Dodges driven by Richard Petty. But the toughest combination to beat in any given race were the Mercurys driven by David Pearson and prepared by Glen and Leonard Wood. Although the three-time NASCAR Winston Cup champion and the Wood Brothers team never ran a full season together, they won 43 races and 51 poles in 143 starts over seven years. Their victories included the 1976 Daytona 500 and two Southern 500s. When Pearson joined the Wood Brothers, the team was running the fastback Mercury Cyclone, but switched to the new Mercury Montego in 1974.

▲ FAST ON AND OFF THE TRACK

As fast as he was on the track, David Pearson benefited from the Wood brothers in the pits. Leonard Wood was the front tire changer on the team that revolutionized pit stops.

◄ TALKING SHOP

The Wood brothers, Glen (left) and Leonard, examined every aspect of racing and developed strategies used to this day.

429-cubic-inch Holman-Moody engine

◄ NO FLAT SPOTS

David Pearson rested the championship trophy on the fender of his crumpled Mercury after driving away from his last-lap accident with Richard Petty in the 1976 Daytona 500.

► MOST FAMOUS FINISH

The Pearson-Petty duel in the 1976 Daytona 500 climaxed when they crashed while battling for the lead coming off the last turn of the race.

Roll bar

Fastback styling

▼ FIT RIVAL FOR A KING

Richard Petty was NASCAR's biggest star when television first covered stock car racing, but the toughest car to beat was the Wood Brothers Mercury driven by David Pearson.

Fuel inlet

Major sponsor

Ehaust header

1975-1980

THE BIG THREE

TELEVISION BEGAN influencing American sports in the early 1950s when baseball and football games were telecast live into homes. Two decades later, however, automobile racing still hadn't made its live television debut. In 1976, ABC aired the finish of the Daytona 500. In a fortuitous moment for stock car racing, the cameras went live as Richard Petty and David Pearson dueled for the lead, then crashed on the final turn. Pearson limped to victory. Three years later, CBS telecast the Daytona 500 live from start to finish. Cale Yarborough and Donnie Allison crashed while battling for the lead with a lap to go. As Richard Petty took the checkered flag, Yarborough and brothers Bobby and Donnie Allison fought in the infield. The network couldn't buy better drama. On cable television, stock car racing became a Sunday regular in living rooms. The competition made for great drama, and interest in NASCAR soared. But the number of models used in stock car racing dwindled as Chrysler slowly withdrew, leaving only Ford and General Motors in NASCAR's Winston Cup Series.

1975-1980 The Ford Thunderbird

FORD FIRST DABBLED with the idea of racing its sporty Thunderbird model in 1959, but didn't until the late 1970s when the factory looked for a racing chassis to replace the Mercury Cyclone and Ford Torino. At first, the Thunderbird struggled. The extended roofline made it suitable for back-seat passengers, but the boxy profile wasn't good for stock car racing. With the Wood Brothers and Bud Moore teams leading development work, Ford tinkered with the design and sloped the rear window in 1983. The Thunderbird became one of the fastest superspeedway cars ever. Thunderbirds won 184 races and carried two drivers to NASCAR Winston Cup championships before being replaced by the Taurus at the beginning of the 1998 season.

▲ END OF THE RUN

Although Ford had already decided to switch to the Taurus in 1998, Thunderbirds won 18 NASCAR Winston Cup races in 1997.

▲ THE BOXY THUNDERBIRD

Neil Bonnett stood next to the Wood Brothers Thunderbird after winning the 1981 Southern 500 at Darlington Raceway. Overall results for Ford teams were not good, as the car's sharp edges inhibited performance.

Contingency sponsors' decals

▼ BEFORE THE T-BIRD

Before the Thunderbird, one of the more aerodynamic cars of the era was the Mercury Cyclone 2+2. With its radically sloped rear deck, the car was popular with racers but not with the public, since the rear seat was virtually unusable.

THUNDERBIRD HIGHLIGHTS

The aerodynamic Thunderbird ran best on the two fastest tracks, Daytona International Speedway and Talladega Superspeedway. Before carburetor restrictor plates lowered speeds, Bill Elliott set records at both tracks that still stand. In 1987 his Thunderbird circled Daytona at 210.364 mph. Later that year his lap at Talladega at 212.809 mph is the fastest in NASCAR history. Thunderbirds claimed 12 poles and won 11 races at Daytona, and had 18 poles and won 12 races at Talladega.

▶ THE YATES BIRD

Former crew chief Robert Yates formed his own team in 1969 and his Thunderbirds won 35 races.

Primary sponsor's decals

▼ AWESOME BILL'S FORD

Bill Elliott won 40 races in Thunderbirds between 1983 and 1994. In 1985 he won 11 superspeedway races. He claimed the first Winston Million by winning the Daytona 500, the Winston 500 at Talladega, and the Southern 500 at Darlington.

Rear deck spoiler

Manufacturer's identification on tire

SCORE

OFF-ROAD RACING'S roots lie in the Southern California deserts. It was there in the 1960s that lightweight, air-cooled engines used in the VW Beetle and Chevrolet Corvair began propelling homemade "buggies" created from steel and chrome-moly tubing. Before long they were racing, and the Southern California Off-Road Enthusiasts was born. Now known simply as SCORE, it sponsors the Baja 1000 and Baja 500. The first Baja 1000 ran in 1967 with a Meyers-Manx modified VW taking 27 hours, 38 minutes to travel from Tijuana to La Paz. In 1998, Ivan Stewart reached La Paz in 19 hours, eight minutes in a modified Toyota pickup. Although the Baja 1000 is open to motorcycles and buggies as well, trucks have led the charge across the desert dry lakes and rocky mountain trails.

▲ IT'S A BIRD

Jason Baldwin got his Ford pickup airborne coming off a jump in the 1998 Baja 1000. The suspensions of off-road trucks allow them to leap over obstacles with little fear of breakage.

▼ TAKES A BEATING

Off-road pickups, such as the Ford driven by Manny Esquerra, are designed for high-speed runs over rough terrain. Speeds on flat surfaces top 110 mph.

Chrome-moly alloy tubing for body

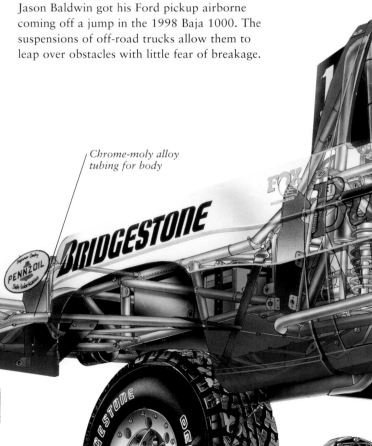

▶ MIGHTY MITE

Roger Mears, the brother of four-time Indy 500 champion Rick Mears, won four season titles driving a Nissan pickup in the SCORE Open Mini-Pickup division.

Rear end housing

DESERT TRUCK CLASSES

Trophy Trucks. Production-based trucks powered by 750-hp V8 engines.

Class 3. Short-wheelbase 4x4 frames.

Class 7S. Stock mini-pickups powered by V4 and V6 engines with two-wheel or four-wheel drive.

Class 7. Stock mini-pickups with V6 engines producing up to 500 hp and open-ended suspension packages.

Class 8. Full-size, two-wheel-drive pickups with 750 hp.V8 engines.

Stock Full. Minimally-altered, full-size American V8 production pickups.

Stock Mini. Minimally-altered mini-pickups with V4 or V6 engines.

Pro Truck. Trucks developed from a template by Ivan Stewart which conform to strict class engine rules.

▶ THE IRON MAN

Toyota and the legendary Ivan "Ironman" Stewart formed one of the great teams in desert racing history. Always driving solo, Stewart won 11 overall championships in the Baja 500 and two more in the Baja 1000.

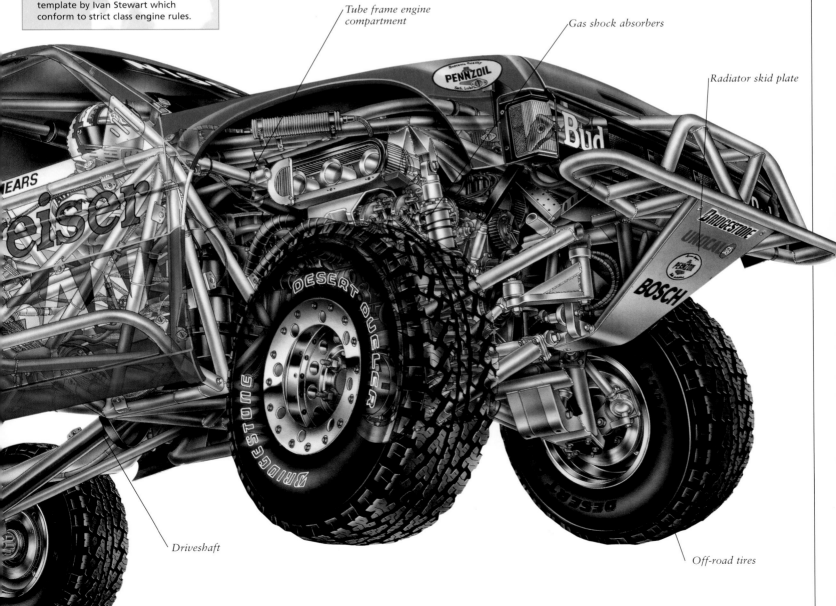

Tube frame engine compartment

Gas shock absorbers

Radiator skid plate

Driveshaft

Off-road tires

1975-1980 Junior Johnson's GM Teams

JUNIOR JOHNSON

NEXT TO PETTY Enterprises, no organization in stock car racing has accounted for more wins than Junior Johnson. As a driver, Johnson is tied for eighth on the all-time list with 50 wins. And as a car owner, his cars won 140 races and claimed 129 poles in 838 events over 31 seasons. It was while fielding General Motors cars for Cale Yarborough and Darrell Waltrip that Johnson reached his zenith as an owner. In 15 seasons from 1972 to 1986, Johnson's General Motors cars captured six Winston Cup titles and finished second six times. Johnson team drivers won 115 races in General Motors equipment between 1971 and 1988.

▲ **DOMINATING DUO**

Cale Yarborough's eight-year association with Junior Johnson resulted in 55 wins, including winning three straight NASCAR Winston Cup championships (1976–78).

▶ **THE PERFECT PACKAGE**

Cale Yarborough stood next to his Chevrolet Monte Carlo after winning the 1977 Daytona 500. He won nine races that season and the second of his record three straight Winston Cup titles in Junior Johnson-owned cars.

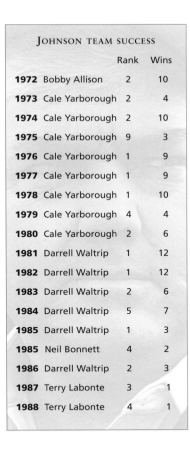

JOHNSON TEAM SUCCESS		
	Rank	Wins
1972 Bobby Allison	2	10
1973 Cale Yarborough	2	4
1974 Cale Yarborough	2	10
1975 Cale Yarborough	9	3
1976 Cale Yarborough	1	9
1977 Cale Yarborough	1	9
1978 Cale Yarborough	1	10
1979 Cale Yarborough	4	4
1980 Cale Yarborough	2	6
1981 Darrell Waltrip	1	12
1982 Darrell Waltrip	1	12
1983 Darrell Waltrip	2	6
1984 Darrell Waltrip	5	7
1985 Darrell Waltrip	1	3
1985 Neil Bonnett	4	2
1986 Darrell Waltrip	2	3
1987 Terry Labonte	3	1
1988 Terry Labonte	4	1

▲ ANOTHER WINNER

Darrell Waltrip pitted his Chevrolet Monte Carlo during the 1986 Daytona 500 in his last season with Junior Johnson.

▶ GREAT START

Junior Johnson's program was at its peak in 1981 and 1982 when Darrell Waltrip won 12 races each season.

103

1975–1980 The Daytona 500

DAYTONA 500
RACE PROGRAM

THE OPENING OF the Daytona International Speedway in 1959 revolutionized stock car racing and introduced a new word into the jargon: superspeedway. Nothing like it existed before Bill France started sculpting his dream from the soft Florida soil. The high-banked turns and tri-oval section made it unique among existing tracks. Even the Indianapolis Motor Speedway looked tame in comparison. Before the inaugural Daytona 500, some drivers feared that cars would fly off the banking and the speeds would create cataclysmic accidents. The reality was just the opposite. Daytona ushered in an era of high speeds and close racing that became the foundation of NASCAR's rapid rise in popularity.

▲ ACKNOWLEDGING TRIUMPH

Dale Earnhardt waved from the cockpit of his Chevrolet Monte Carlo as he took the checkered flag to win the 1998 Daytona 500.

◄ THE ALLISON 500

One of the greatest finishes in Daytona 500 history came in 1988 when Bobby Allison won just ahead of son Davey.

◄ PEARSON VS. PETTY

The battles between Richard Petty and David Pearson at Daytona became one of the richest chapters in stock car folklore.

DAYTONA BEACH MORNING JOURNAL 10¢

DAYTONA BEACH, FLORIDA, MONDAY, FEBRUARY 24, 1964

Richard Petty Wins It BIG

Like Father, Like Son:
Richard Wins The 500

Plymouth Rock
The Melody For
Petty Runaway

◄A FAMILY AFFAIR

Richard Petty won the 1964 Daytona 500 by more than a lap five years after his father, Lee, won the inaugural in a photo finish.

▼RACE WITHIN THE RACE

Joe Nemechek's crew refueled and changed the right side tires on the Bell South Chevy Monte Carlo during a pit stop in the 1998 Daytona 500.

DAYTONA

START/FINISH

The diagram of Daytona International Speedway has become one of the best known profiles in racing. The pit lane bisects the tri-oval section that includes the start-finish line. The infield section of the road course is just beyond the pit lane exit. Dirt removed from the infield to build the banking created Lake Lloyd.

1975-1980 Modern Marvels

MECHANICS HAVE ALWAYS looked for ways to make a car go faster. Put a set of rules in front of a crew chief and he'll look for a way to bend or stretch the regulations. The legends of Junior Johnson and Smokey Yunick grew largely from their ability to stay a step ahead of the tech police. "I loved the game," Johnson once said. "Maybe I'd have four or five new things on a car that might raise a question. But I'd always leave something that was outside of the regulations in a place where the inspectors could easily find it. They'd tell me it was illegal, I'd plead guilty, and they'd carry it away thinking they caught me. But they didn't check some other things that I thought were even more special." Some cars have driven through huge loopholes in the rules. Other cars, like Buddy Baker's 1980 Oldsmobile Cutlass were fast because crew chiefs and drivers hit on combinations first. Some, like Johnson's famed banana car, forced NASCAR to rewrite the rule book.

▲ DRIVING THROUGH A LOOPHOLE

Before the 1981 season, NASCAR went to smaller models for its Winston Cup cars. Some teams laughed at the Pontiac Le Mans, believing it couldn't compete. Bobby Allison's Le Mans (right) won the pole at the Daytona 500 and finished second in the race.

▲ THE BANANA REVOLUTION

Officially it was a Ford Torino, but Junior Johnson lowered the roofline so much the driver had to slide into his seat. The bright yellow color had rivals calling it the Banana Car and Flying Banana. Fred Lorenzen led the 1966 Atlanta 500 until he crashed.

▶ THE GRAY GHOST

Crew chief Waddell Wilson found the perfect car for the right driver in the Olds Cutlass he built for Buddy Baker in 1980. The car's gray color made it hard to see on the long backstretches.

Factory standard front bumper

▲ **THE TOTAL PACKAGE**

Jeff Gordon's Chevrolet Monte Carlo was one of the most dominant cars in NASCAR Winston Cup history. From 1995 to 1998, his team won three titles and was second once. Gordon won 40 times in 127 starts, with 70 top-three finishes.

▲ **UNIQUE WINNER**

In 1985, Bill Gardner's crew chief Gary Nelson built a Chevrolet using engine parts, shock absorbers, and other parts that NASCAR wanted to test. It won the Pepsi Firecracker 400 at Daytona International Speedway.

Drivers safety net

Fastback design

Rear spoiler

Side exhaust

1975-1980 The Chevy Evolution

CHEVROLET EMBLEM

IN 1971 RICHARD HOWARD, president of Charlotte Motor Speedway, asked Junior Johnson to build a Chevrolet to race in the World 600. Chevrolet was not racing then, and Howard wanted a Chevy in his race. Johnson used the Monte Carlo as the body style, and it became a Winston Cup regular the next year. In 1973, Benny Parsons drove one to its first Winston Cup title, and nearly 30 years later it has won more races than any model in Winston Cup history. The 2000 Monte Carlo bears little resemblance to that 1971 prototype. The original boxy design gave way to the Lumina as Chevy's racing model in 1989. When the Monte Carlo returned in 1994, its sharp corners had been rounded. Overall, Monte Carlos have won more than 35 percent of the races they have started.

▲ EARLY MONTE CARLOS

Lennie Pond (No. 54) and James Hylton (No. 48) battled on the high banks of Daytona International Speedway in matched Monte Carlos in 1975.

▼ FIRST CHAPTER

Chevrolet was taking a hard look at the aging Monte Carlo design when Darrell Waltrip was running the venerable model in 1987.

▲ FIRST MONTE CARLO WINNER

Powered by the 427-cubic-inch Chevrolet V8, Bobby Allison scored the Monte Carlo's first victory on March 26, 1972, in the Atlanta 500.

◄ TEAMMATE TRAIN

Neil Bonnett (No. 12) led teammate Darrell Waltrip (No. 11) in a 1985 duel between Monte Carlo SS models fielded by Junior Johnson.

▼ LUMINA STAR

From 1989 through 1994, Chevy ran the sleeker Lumina as its Winston Cup car. Sterling Marlin's Lumina (No. 4) won the 1994 Daytona 500.

► EARNHARDT RULES

Dale Earnhardt won his first Daytona 500 in a Monte Carlo in 1998. Twenty-five different drivers have won races in Monte Carlos.

In the Garage

1975-1980

SPEEDWAY GARAGES

BURNING THE MIDNIGHT oil isn't just a cliché during race weekends. Completing tasks on multiple-page checklists is routine business for crew members who put in long shifts. When something goes wrong, like a blown engine or an accident, the work multiplies. NASCAR sets flexible time limits, which are bent if a team needs extra time to repair a damaged car. The garage is the hub of crew life. Crew members eat and relax there as well as work on race weekends. The garage becomes a weekend home, with furnishings that include tools as well as lounge chairs.

▲ QUICK FIX

Until 1984, teams were allowed to change engines during a race. The Petty Enterprises team led by crew chief Dale Inman boasted it could change an engine in 20 minutes.

▶ TIGHT FIT

A 750-hp V8 engine was guided into Dale Earnhardt's Chevrolet.

▼ BEHIND THE SCENES

Much of the prerace preparation work is done far from the track. While a team is at one site for a race weekend, most of the crew remains at the shop preparing engines and cars for future races.

Crews once worked at a more leisurely pace. This team repaired the cooling system during a post-war race on the Beach-Road course at Daytona Beach, Florida.

▲ **BEHIND THE WALL**

Small problems during a race are fixed on pit row. Big ones require moving the car behind the inside pit wall. Jack Roush's crew assessed Ted Musgrave's damaged Ford at Texas Motor Speedway in 1998.

▼ **OFFICIAL BUSINESS**

Years ago, inspectors visited this Mercury on the Beach-Road course at Daytona Beach, Florida. Today, long lines snake through the garages as cars come to the inspection teams.

▼ **CHOREOGRAPHED ACTION**

The Morgan-McClure crew made routine adjustments to the Chevrolet Monte Carlo of Bobby Hamilton during practice for the 1998 spring race at Bristol, Tennessee.

1980-1990

PRIME TIME

RICHARD PETTY WON his record 200th, and last, Winston Cup race on July 4, 1987, at Daytona International Speedway. It was the culminating victory for NASCAR's old guard, most of whom had left during the 1980s. (David Pearson retired in 1986 and Bobby Allison and Cale Yarborough quit two years later, but Petty drove until 1992.) A new group of champions was taking over. In 1979 Dale Earnhardt was Rookie of the Year on the Winston Cup circuit. A year later, he won his first of seven Winston Cup titles. Darrell Waltrip won titles the next two seasons in Junior Johnson's Buicks and won another in 1985 in a Chevrolet. The cameras loved Waltrip and fans loved what they saw of the new breed, in particular Earnhardt, who followed Waltrip with titles for Chevy in 1986 and 1987. Geoff Bodine, Bill Elliott, Terry Labonte, Mark Martin, Ricky Rudd, and Rusty Wallace all became winners in the fast and furious 1980s. Martin, a four-time champion, came to NASCAR from the ASA series. Bodine had raced in NASCAR's Modified Division. And Wally Dallenbach moved into Winston Cup cars after winning two straight Trans-Am titles.

1980-1990 Reining in the Horses

MODERN RESTRICTOR PLATE

CARBURETOR RESTRICTOR plates were used to limit speeds during the early 1970s. NASCAR eliminated them in 1979 and then downsized body styles two years later, and speeds rose. In 1978 Cale Yarborough won the pole for the Daytona 500 with a speed of 187.536 mph in an Olds 88. By 1987 at Talladega, Bill Elliott's Thunderbird qualified at a record 212.809 mph. Then Bobby Allison was nearly killed in a horrific crash. Restrictor plates returned. Speeds fell and a new term came into the language of racing at Daytona and Talladega – pack racing.

▲ ROUNDING OFF THE EDGES

Speed is escalating again on Winston Cup tracks, but with restrictor plates limiting horsepower, the focus is on aerodynamics.

◄ THE RULES HAVE CHANGED

Bill Elliott posed in front of the Ford Thunderbird that he drove to the fastest qualifying time in stock car history before the Winston 500 at Talladega Superspeedway in 1987. Elliott lapped the 2.66-mile track at 212.809 mph.

WORLD'S FASTEST RACE CAR

Daytona 500

▼ RICK HENDRICK'S DREAM FINISH

The 1997 Daytona 500 marked the first time in race history that a team finished 1-2-3. The cars were Chevrolet Monte Carlos owned by Rick Hendrick. Jeff Gordon (right) won, followed by Terry Labonte (middle) and Ricky Craven.

▼ THE PACK ATTACK

In restrictor plate races, speeds are almost equal across the field. Because horsepower is restricted, there is little need to brake on the high-banked superspeedways.

▼ T-BIRD TANDEM

The Ford Thunderbirds of Bill Elliott (right) and Davey Allison led the pack at the start of the 1987 Daytona 500. Elliott won both the pole (with a track-record lap of 210.364 mph) and the race in the last Daytona 500 run before restrictor plates.

1980-1990 Sponsors

MONEY MAKES THE cars go, and prize money is just a drop in the bucket. Stock car teams need sponsors to pay the bills. It costs at least $6 million a year to race. The main sponsor may spend up to $10 million. Secondary and associate sponsors bring $250,000 to $500,000 apiece. Years ago a sponsor might be the local garage that supplied labor, parts, or tires. Early factory teams shared space on their cars with local dealerships. Holly Farms Chicken became one of the first non-automotive sponsors with Junior Johnson in the early 1960s. Later, Gatorade painted a bottle label on Donnie Allison's car. Buddy Arrington drove a Dodge sponsored by a Ford dealership. Lake Speed drove a Chevy painted like a tin of Spam. Wrangler used Dale Earnhardt's "tough customer" image to sell jeans.

▼ EARLY RACE SPONSOR

Although Pure Premium products sponsored this 1953 race, it would be 10 years before sponsors' names began appearing in official race titles.

◄ LEGAL LIQUID

The sport which once drew many drivers from the moonshining business now found soft drink sponsorships to pay the bills.

▼ WINNING COMBINATION

Pontiac and GM Goodwrench Services have been with drag racing Pro Stock driver Warren Johnson since 1988.

Support sponsor

▼ SIMPLE MESSAGE

Stock cars were still relatively clean of labels in the early 1970s. Fred Lorenzen bore the STP on his Plymouth Roadrunner in 1971.

▼ PERFECT FINISH

The sponsors got maximum exposure when Rick Hendrick's team swept the top three spots in the 1997 Daytona 500. From left are Terry Labonte (second), Jeff Gordon (first), and Ricky Craven (third).

▼ MORE THAN A CAR

True Value Hardware Stores annually sponsors all 12 cars that run in the four-race International Race of Champions Series.

Secondary sponsor

▶ PIT BOARD

Putting the sponsor's name on the pit row identification board is a novel way to get the message out.

Dodge Avenger model sponsor

Series sponsor

1980-1990 Paint Design

THE ORIGINAL COLOR of most stock cars was black, but distinctive paint patterns quickly became a part of the scene. Even with numbers on the doors, teams had a hard time identifying cars in the dust on early tracks, and colors attracted the spectator's eye to certain cars and sponsors. Soon a rainbow of colors appeared, except for green, which racers saw as unlucky until Gatorade became a major sponsor and demanded its cars be green to match the label on its bottles. Since then, design has been a factor of paint jobs – as in the Bullseye Barbecue Sauce pattern on Sterling Marlin's Chevy. Cars began to look like boxes of detergent and corn flakes. One-race schemes appeared, and soon they had become so wild that numbers were hard to read, but the sponsor was easily identifiable.

▲ PAINT BY NUMBERS

Many early paint jobs evolved from a last-minute decision to make the roof, hood, or fenders a different color so the car would be easier to spot from the pits and by the scorers who counted the laps.

Air intake

Manufacturer logo

◄ NOT LIKELY

While paint designs are meant to attract attention, rival drivers, at least, were likely to ignore this plea.

▼ NOT A GOOD DAY

Fred Flintstone and Dino the Dinosaur looked hurt when Wally Dallenbach was involved in a crash in the Cartoon Network Ford.

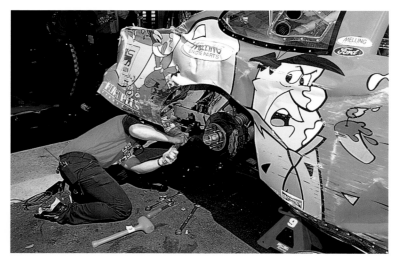

▲ SIMPLE BUT EFFECTIVE

Paint design has changed radically since Dale Earnhardt ran the Cardinal Tractor Co. Chevy Monte Carlo in 1979.

◄**PRODUCT IDENTIFICATION**

The hood of every car belongs to the primary sponsor. Usually, the emblem of the car make is also included in the design.

▲ **EVERYONE KNOWS NO. 3**

Fans know it as Dale Earnhardt's number, but it actually belongs to owner Richard Childress. NASCAR numbers stay with a team as long as it races.

▼ **SALESMEN**

Terry Labonte in the Kellogg's Chevy Monte Carlo led the Valvoline Ford Taurus driven by Mark Martin.

▲ **FASTER THAN A SPEEDING BULLET**

Usually in the rainbow pattern of DuPont Automotive finishes, Jeff Gordon ran a promotion featuring Superman on the side of his Chevrolet Monte Carlo.

1980-1990 Earnhardt's Chevys

DALE EARNHARDT is a Chevy man. His first win came in a Monte Carlo owned by Rod Osterlund in the 1979 Southeastern 500 at Bristol, Tennessee. Each of his seven Winston Cup titles has come in a Chevy, as have all but three of his career wins. Earnhardt is the only driver with more than 70 wins for Chevrolet. He ranks first in wins in the Lumina model. Four of his Winston Cup titles came during the five-season run of the Lumina. His father, Ralph, was a champion NASCAR short-track driver whose strong will earned him the nickname "Ironheart." Dale developed a hard-nosed driving style that earned him the nickname "The Intimidator."

▲ LUMINOUS RESULTS

Between 1989 and 1994, Chevrolet ran the Lumina model. Earnhardt won four Winston Cup titles and 27 of the 61 wins scored by the Lumina.

Richard Petty

▼ No. 1 AGAIN

Dale Earnhardt posed by his Monte Carlo after tying Richard Petty's record with his seventh Winston Cup title in 1994. He was voted the national Driver of the Year after winning 10 races and scoring 21 top-five finishes. His points margin was the fifth-widest in history.

◄ **THE SECOND GENERATION**

When Chevy replaced the Lumina model with the newer and sleeker Monte Carlo for the start of the 1995 season, Dale Earnhardt went along for the ride.

▼ **FINALLY!**

Two decades of frustration ended in 1998 when Dale Earnhardt won his first Daytona 500.

▼ **WRANGLING A TITLE**

Dale Earnhardt (No. 3), overtook Richard Petty to win the race at Charlotte. Earnhardt swept both Charlotte races and won his first NASCAR Winston Cup championship with car owner Richard Childress in 1986.

Dale Earnhardt

1980-1990 Twists and Turns: Road Courses

FIRST DAYTONA BEACH RACE IN 1936

THE OVAL IS the backbone of stock car racing, but road racing was part of the sport even before NASCAR was formed. The most famous traditional stock car circuit was the Beach-Road course at Daytona Beach, Florida. NASCAR's first road race was held on the runways of Linden Airport in Linden, New Jersey, on June 13, 1954. It was the only NASCAR race won by a foreign car – the Jaguar of Al Keller. The road course became a part of the NASCAR schedule in 1957 when the tour went to Watkins Glen, New York. Today only Watkins Glen and Sears Point Raceway in Sonoma, California, remain on the schedule. Rusty Wallace and Bobby Allison share the record with six wins apiece on road courses.

▲ LIKE AN OVAL

The last turn onto the main straight and the start-finish line at Sears Point Raceway has been the site of several incidents since the track north of San Francisco joined the schedule in 1989.

▼ S–TURNS

The series of bends at Riverside Raceway, California, became known as "the esses." Richard Petty was famous for cutting across the dirt and turning the esses into a semi-straightaway.

WATKINS GLEN

← START/FINISH

Located near a small town in the finger lakes region of upstate New York, Watkins Glen is one of the more famous tracks in American motorsports history. The former home of the U.S. Formula One Grand Prix, Watkins Glen has hosted endurance races and NASCAR Winston Cup races over the years. NASCAR first visited Watkins Glen in 1957, returned in 1964–65, and came back in 1986 to stay.

◄ROAD READY

Changes in elevation as well as left and right turns force stock car teams to work overtime preparing a car for road courses.

▼MASTERING THE ART

Dale Earnhardt, who led at the top of the turn three hill, took road racing lessons before winning his only road race in 1995 at Sears Point.

SEARS POINT

START/FINISH

The 1.949-mile, 12-turn course at Sears Point has a drag strip running parallel to the back section of the track. Surrounded by vineyards, the track, in the heart of northern California's wine country, is one of the more scenic racing venues in the Western Hemisphere.

1980-1990 The Busch Grand National

FOR SOME DRIVERS, it is a stepping-stone, for others, a career. Fans know it as the Busch Grand National, NASCAR's second-echelon series to the Winston Cup. Although Ned Jarrett remains the only Grand National champion (1957–58) to become a Winston Cup champion (1961 and 1965), others have honed their skills in less-powerful Grand National cars before jumping to the Winston Cup. Saturday afternoons often find Winston Cup drivers moonlighting in Grand National races. A Winston Cup driver, Mark Martin, is the division's all-time leader in wins. But the Grand National was also home to legends like Red Farmer, Jack Ingram, Sam Ard, and Randy LaJoie. Martin became the first Grand National driver to reach the 40-win plateau in 1990. Ingram, with five season championships, is second with 31 wins, followed by Tommy Houston (24), and Ard and Tommy Ellis tied for fifth with 22 wins apiece.

▲ **TWO OF THE GREATS**

The Pontiacs of Jack Ingram (No. 11) and Tommy Ellis (No. 4) battled in the only Grand National race run at Asheville, North Carolina, in May 1982. Ingram won and Ellis finished second.

ALL-TIME GRAND NATIONAL CHAMPIONSHIP LEADERS	
Driver	Titles
1. Jack Ingram	5
2. Rene Charland	4
3. Red Farmer	3
Mike Klapak	3
5. Sam Ard	2
Dale Earnhardt Jr.	2
Ned Jarrett	2
Randy LaJoie	2
Butch Lindley	2
L. D. Ottinger	2
Larry Pearson	2

▶ **FUTURE CHAMP**

The Buick driven by two-time Busch Grand National champ Randy LaJoie (No. 07) moved inside the Pontiac driven by Chuck Bown (No. 7).

► **ALL-TIME LEADER**

Mark Martin had just won three straight American Speed Association championships when he debuted in this Chevy Monte Carlo on the 1982 Grand National tour.

▲ **GROUND FLOOR**

Future Winston Cup champion Dale Jarrett posed next to the Mercury Capri that he raced in 1981 in NASCAR's Dash Series for four-cylinder cars. The Dash Series is a stepping-stone to NASCAR's Grand National and Craftsman Trucks divisions.

Windshield support strips

Grille with air intakes

Tires outside quarter panel

1980-1990 IROC

EVERY SPORT HAS an all-star game, and that was the idea behind the formation of the International Race of Champions in 1973. A dozen of the world's top drivers compete in identical cars over a four-race series. The formula led to very exciting and close finishes with the determining factor being driver skill. A team of 25 mechanics, fabricators, and shop workers keeps the cars equal. The 1974 series raced in Porsche Carrera RSRs. Chevrolet Camaros were used from 1975 to 1989, and introduced two specialty models, the Z-28 and IROC. Dodges were run from 1990 to 1995, the Daytona for the first four years and then the Avenger. Since 1996, the IROC car has been the Pontiac Firebird with a small-block, 350-cubic-inch General Motors V8 producing 500 hp at 6,800 rpm.

DAVID PEARSON LED A. J. FOYT IN THE FIRST IROC SERIES

▲ **FLYING FIREBIRDS**

Pontiac has supplied Firebirds for the IROC series since 1996. Dale Earnhardt passed Greg Ray during the 2000 heat at Daytona International Speedway.

▲ **FINALE FOR DONOHUE**

Mark Donohue led George Follmer at Daytona International Speedway. He won three of the four races to win the first IROC series, run in Porsche Carrera RSRs in 1974.

▲ **TIGHT QUARTERS**

All 12 Dodge Daytonas racing in the 1991 IROC dueled for the lead 12 laps into the Daytona International Speedway opener of the four-race set. Scott Pruett (No. 5) won the race but the series title went to Rusty Wallace, who was last at this junction.

Air intakes

▲ CLASSIC CAMAROS

The Chevrolet Camaro was used in the IROC series from 1975 through 1989. The IROC Z-28 was used in 1987 when Geoff Bodine won the title.

IROC HIGHLIGHTS

1974 Mark Donohue wins three of four races in Porsche Carrera and first title.

1975 A. J. Foyt wins title without winning any of the eight races.

1986 Al Unser Jr. becomes IROC champion and joins father Al and uncle Bobby as Unsers to win IROC races.

1990 Dale Earnhardt wins his first IROC title.

1994 Mark Martin wins IROC title in first year for Dodge Avenger.

1996 Martin wins first of three straight IROC titles as Pontiac Firebird joins series.

1999 Dale Earnhardt wins third IROC title and Mark Martin is first driver to win ten IROC races.

1980-1990 International

*TOYOTA COROLLA
OFF-ROAD RALLY RACER*

OUTSIDE THE BORDERS of the United States, off-road racing is called rallying. Although the two disciplines have a different set of rules, both put driver and vehicle to the ultimate endurance test. While off-road races are normally point-to-point, non-stop events of up to 1,000 miles, international rallies are conducted in daily stages that can extend over weeks, as in the instance of the famed Paris-to-Dakkar rally. Championship rally drivers match their cars against a variety of conditions and obstacles. Among the top rally drivers right now is Finland's Tommi Makinen, who has won four straight WRC titles driving a Mitsubishi Lancer Evolution IV.

▲ POWERFUL PACKAGE

Boosted by a twin-scroll turbocharger and high-capacity intercooler, the four-cylinder engine on the World Rally Champion Mitsubishi Lancer Evolution boosts rallying's top power-to-weight ratio. Tommi Makinen powered his Mitsubishi through a stream bed in Portugal.

► FOUR-WHEEL FLYER

Great Britain's Richard Burns got his four-cylinder Subaru Imprezza totally off the ground during the 1999 Portugal Rally.

France's Gerard Dillman slid his VW Beetle through an icy turn at the annual Trophee Andros Rallye at Val Thorens, France.

▼ **TOUGH SLEDDING**

Marcel Tarres tested the limits of his Citroen Xsara on a snowy slope during the 1999 Trophee Andros Rallye at Val Thorens, France.

▼ **WINNING COMBINATION**

The Finnish driving team of Tommi Makinen and Risto Mannisenmaki in the Mitsubishi Lancer Evolution charged along a dusty forest path east of Perth, Australia. They won four straight World Rally Championships from 1996 to 1999.

1990-2000

SMART CARS, NEW HORIZONS

THE LAST RACE of the 1992 season at Atlanta, Georgia, represented a milestone in NASCAR Winston Cup history. It was the last race driven by Richard Petty and the Winston Cup debut of Jeff Gordon. The changing of the guard was one of the many changes in stock car racing during the decade of the '90s. Cars got sleeker. Chevrolet replaced the Lumina with the new Monte Carlo. Ford followed, replacing the Thunderbird with the Taurus. Before the 2000 season, the profiles of both the Monte Carlo and Taurus were faired again. "Aerodynamics" replaced "drafting" as the bellweather word in stock car racing. Purses soared as NASCAR signed its first comprehensive television package. Meanwhile the striking gains spread to other forms of stock car racing. The Craftsman Truck Series was launched in 1995. New superspeedways opened in Texas, Las Vegas, Nevada, Southern California, and South Florida. And the Trans-Am Series expanded with the introduction of foreign models after Tom Kendall capped a three-year run at the top of the series standings by winning a record 11 straight races in 1997.

◄ **TITLE FORM**

Dale Jarrett stops his Ford Taurus in perfect position as the Robert Yates crew goes to work during a routine pit stop. Teamwork led Jarrett to the 1999 NASCAR Winston Cup title.

▼ **POTENT PICKUP**

Packing the power of a Winston Cup car, the Ford driven on the Craftsman Truck Series by Mike Wallace is less aerodynamic than a car, making it tougher to handle.

1990-2000 Drag Racing

ALTHOUGH THE NITRO-burning Top Fuel and Funny Car classes grab the headlines, one of the most popular professional classes in drag racing is Pro Stock. Pro Stock is the modern extension of grassroots drag racing. This fierce competition between production-based street hot rods is colorful and spectacular. Automotive factories are heavily involved in Pro Stock and Pro Stock Truck, with Ford, Pontiac, Buick, Oldsmobile, and Dodge competing in the division over the years.

▶ GM MAN

Warren Johnson started his Pro Stock career in an Oldsmobile before shifting to Pontiac. Early in 2000, the five-time champion became the third driver in NHRA history to win 80 events.

Two 4-barrel carburetors

Radiator

Fiberglass body

▲ LARGE FOR A FINGER

Super Gas driver Jim Picco of Modesto, California, calls his 1966 Chevy Chevelle "Debby's Ring" in tribute to the sacrifices necessary for a husband-wife team to field a car.

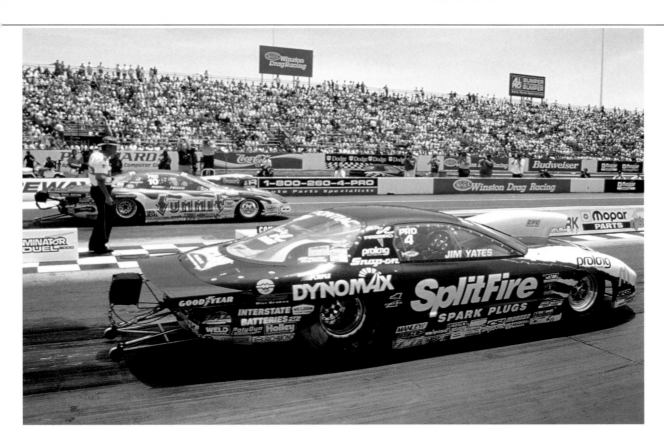

Jim Yates drove a
Pontiac to back-to-back
NHRA Pro Stock season
championships in
1996–97. Nine of his 22
event wins came in
1997.

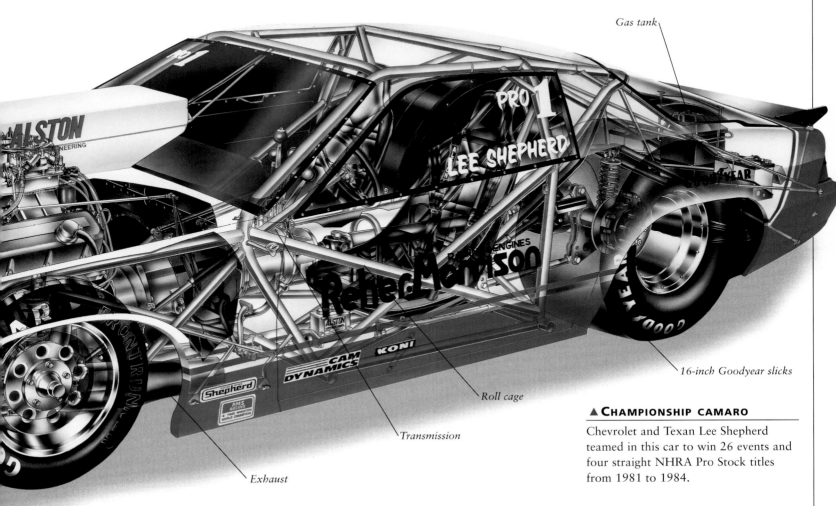

Gas tank

PRO 1

LEE SHEPHERD

16-inch Goodyear slicks

Roll cage

Transmission

Exhaust

▲ **CHAMPIONSHIP CAMARO**

Chevrolet and Texan Lee Shepherd
teamed in this car to win 26 events and
four straight NHRA Pro Stock titles
from 1981 to 1984.

1990-2000 TRANS-AM'S New Leaders

FOR THE TRANS-AM Series, the ebb and flow of racing has been a wild ride. After the pony car wars of the late 1960s the series almost died. By the mid-1980s interest soared in the new drivers and new cars. Wally Dallenbach Jr. won titles in 1985 and 1986 in a Mercury Capri and Chevrolet Camaro. Future IndyCar and Winston Cup driver Scott Pruett won with a Mercury Merkur XR4Ti. Hurley Haywood took the championship in 1988 in an Audi Quattro. Then, beween 1990 and 1997, Tom Kendall won four series titles and 26 races. Paul Gentilozzi won titles in 1998–1999 in a Chevrolet Corvette and a Mustang, then switched to a Jaguar for the 2000 season. Three-time series runner-up Brian Simo went from a Mustang to a DiTomaso Mangusta. Olds Auroras and Cutlasses, Chevy Camaros and Corvettes, and Ford Mustang Cobras also campaigned.

▲ THE BIG CAT

Ford's acquisition of Jaguar led two-time Trans-Am champion Paul Gentilozzi to switch from a Mustang Cobra to the Jaguar XKR for the 2000 series.

◄ MUCHO GUSTO

Brian Simo switched to a Qvale DiTomaso Mangusta for the 2000 season and won the first two races.

Rear wing

Extended rear deck

Radio antennas

Camera

▼ BEST OF BOTH

A Trans-Am road racer is a cross between a Winston Cup car and an endurance sports car. Chevrolet teams run Monte Carlos on the Winston Cup curcuit, Corvettes and Camaros (Ken Murillo's shown here) in Trans-Am. Ford runs Tauruses in Winston Cup competition and Mustang Cobras in the Trans-Am.

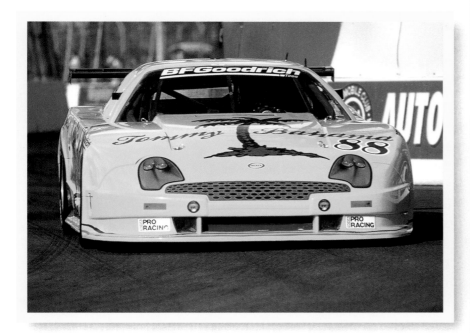

TRANS-AM WINS BY MODEL

1. Ford Mustang		95
2. Chevrolet Camaro		88
3. Chevrolet Corvette		47
4. Porsche 911		38
5. Mercury Capri		25

▲ STREET SCENE

The Trans-Am Series is run entirely on road courses and temporary street circuits. G. J. Mennen's Chevrolet Camaro negotiated Long Beach, California's tight turns during the 2000 race.

Front quarter panel

◄ DIFFERENT BREED

Johnny Miller's Trans-Am Chevrolet Corvette is strikingly different from a Winston Cup car. Most notable are the lower profile, rear wing, enlarged quarter panels, and sloped rear window.

Front air dam

The Transporter: A Traveling Shop

LIVING QUARTERS

THE RIGS THAT haul cars to and from races also double as the team's operations center for race weekends. Packed inside those trailers is everything a team will need for a race. And once it is unloaded at the track, the spotless interior of the trailer becomes a team lounge and office. The only things not carried in the trailer are wheels, tires, and fuel – three items supplied at the track. The truck drivers are responsible for the truck's inventory as well as getting it to the track on time. They pack, driving, and unpack in a cycle repeated more than 44 times a year. The average Winston Cup transporter travels about 70,000 miles in a racing season.

▲ HUMBLE BEGINNINGS

In the early days of NASCAR's Winston Cup Series, crew chiefs pulled cars to the track on open trailers hitched to the family sedan or pickup truck. This is how Smokey Yunick's Chevrolet Chevelle arrived at the track.

Wind deflector

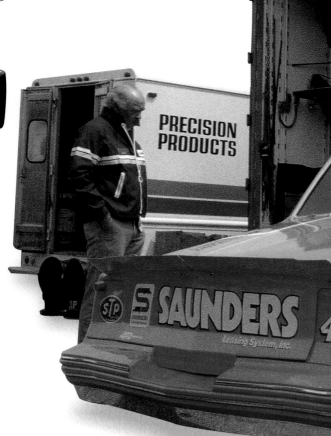

▲ MOBILE HOME

A transporter includes living quarters for the two-driver teams who often have to shuttle cars from coast to coast in just over two days.

◄ **HUB OF ACTIVITY**

On race weekend, the trailer is a command post and a hospitality center for guests, friends, and family members. At the end of the race, it takes a team less than a half hour to repack and hit the road.

▼ **EVERYTHING IN ITS PLACE**

Each NASCAR Winston Cup team travels with two cars in its transporter. Both are carried on a platform at the top of the hauler.

Extra car

Loading ramp

1990-2000 Gordon's Chevys

GORDON'S NUMBER

JEFF GORDON and his Rainbow Warriors crew changed the look of NASCAR Winston Cup racing in the 1990s. Driving Chevrolets owned by Rick Hendrick, Gordon won 48 races and three Winston Cup titles from 1994 through 1999 and played a prominent role as the Winston Cup's popularity hit record highs. Gordon, who, at the age of 24 in 1995, was the youngest champion of the Winston Cup's modern era, was blessed with the combination of great driving skills and matinee idol looks – making him the favorite of the younger and diverse fans tuning into Winston Cup racing. Teams scrambled to find the "next" Gordon, opening the door for another young charger – Tony Stewart.

Roll cage

Communications antenna

Aerodynamic front end

▲ SHAPED FOR SPEED

The rounded nose on the DuPont Chevy Monte Carlo shows the latest thinking in aerodynamic design. The low front spoiler reduces the amount of air flowing beneath the car while the rounded nose creates a smoother entry.

▼ SOLID BRAINTRUST

Gordon's rapid rise in Winston Cup racing was a team effort that included car owner Rick Hendrick (left) and crew chief Ray Evernham.

▼ THE RECORD PACE

As he neared becoming the first driver in Winston Cup history to win 50 races before his 30th birthday, Gordon had a winning percentage of 21 percent – the highest mark among drivers with ten or more career wins.

◀ VICTORY AT THE PINNACLE

Jeff Gordon's Chevy Monte Carlo led the pack after a restart en route to victory in the 1999 Daytona 500.

▼ WINNING A FORTUNE

Victory in the 1999 Daytona 500 also reaped Gordon a $1 million bonus from Winston's No Bull Five program.

HENDRICK TEAM HIGHLIGHTS

1984	Fields first car in NASCAR Winston Cup Series and wins three races with Geoff Bodine as driver.
1986	Campaigns two cars for the first time with Bodine and Tim Richmond as drivers; Richmond wins seven races and finishes third in final standings.
1987	Fields three-car team with Bodine, Benny Parsons, and Darrell Waltrip as primary drivers; also enters fourth car for Richmond in eight races.
1989	Waltrip wins six races and finishes fourth in points.
1991	Ricky Rudd finishes second in season standings.
1992	Jeff Gordon debuts with team in final race of season.
1993	Gordon is Winston Cup Rookie of the Year.
1995	Gordon wins seven races and becomes youngest Winston Cup champion of modern era.
1996	Teammates Terry Labonte and Gordon finish 1-2, respectively, in final standings.
1997	Gordon wins ten races for second straight year and wins Winston Cup title.
1998	Gordon equals modern era record for 13 wins in a season and wins third Winston Cup title.

1990-2000 The Craftsman Truck Series

IN THE EARLY 1990s, pickup trucks, long the chariot of the American workman, became popular with younger buyers, including women. NASCAR noticed the number of trucks in the parking lots of their events. In 1993, NASCAR commissioned off-road enthusiasts Jimmy Smith, Jim Venable, Dick Landfield, and Frank Vessels to build a prototype pickup truck suitable for racing on asphalt ovals. In 1995, the new Craftsman Truck Series was launched. The tour quickly found its niche as NASCAR's third nationally-recognized series. Chevrolets won the first five championships.

▲ THROWBACK

The Ford F-150 driven by Tony Raines in 1998 was a close cousin to the Ford Taurus run on the Winston Cup circuit. Both were powered by 351-cubic-inch Ford V8 engines.

Front air dam

▲ PACK ATTACK

NASCAR's Craftsman Truck Series won many fans due to the boxier design of the trucks, which allows drivers to draft and make ion slingshot passes.

◄ DOOR TO DOOR

The sight of Scott Hansen's Chevy (left) swapping paint with Mike Stefanik's Ford at Martinsville, Virginia, in 1999 was not unusual in Craftsman Truck racing.

▲ TRUCKS ARRIVE

The Craftsman Truck Series first raced at Daytona International Speedway's tri-oval on February 18, 2000. Kurt Busch (No. 99), Greg Biffle (No. 50), Kenny Martin (No. 98), and Dennis Setzer (No. 1) battled for the lead but Mike Wallace won in a Ford with Busch second.

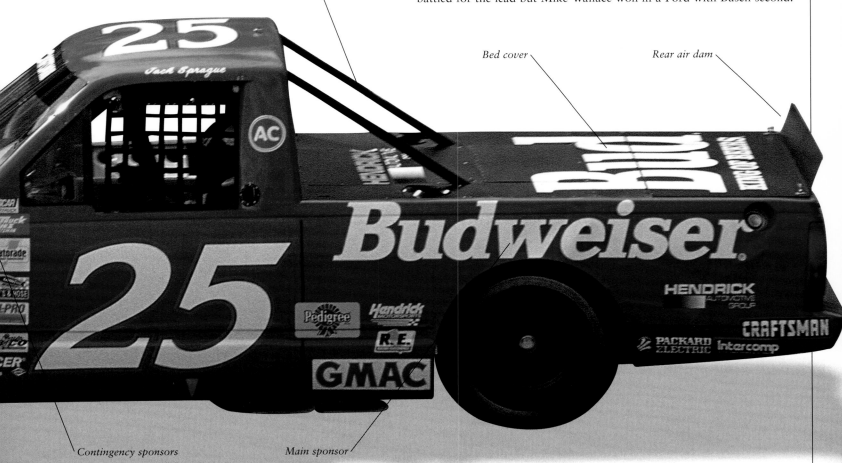

Roll cage extension to strengthen bed

Bed cover

Rear air dam

Contingency sponsors

Main sponsor

▲ DEPENDABLE PACKAGE

Jack Sprague was the only driver to start every race through the first five years of the NASCAR Craftsman Truck Series. The Chevy driver also won two truck titles.

1990-2000

The Pit Crew

NASCAR PIT CREW MEMBER

TO THE UNINFORMED, the pit stop looks chaotic. But the work performed by the six-member "over the wall" teams in five or six 15-second bursts during a stock car race can be as crucial as anything the driver does. A typical crew member's day begins early in the morning with preparation of the car and ends late at night with the storing of equipment. Great pit stops might account for the margin of victory. Good ones will keep a driver in the hunt. Bad ones doom a team to a poor result as surely as a brush with the wall. Each crew member has an assigned task. The driver also plays a role – stopping the car on the marks, then accelerating away smoothly when the work is done.

▲ RIGHT SIDE ONLY

The Valvoline team completed a right-side-only tire change on Mark Martin's Ford at Daytona International Speedway.

Gas can

▲ PENALTY BOX

Each pit stall is a box marked by white lines. All four tires of the car must be inside the lines when the crew goes to work. A violation can result in a 15-second penalty.

Air wrench

◀ **THERE IS A PLAN**

At Virginia's Martinsville Speedway, Mike Skinner's Chevrolet negotiated the narrow access lane to the garage area.

▼ **INSIDE OUT**

In contrast to Winston Cup races, the refueling nozzle on road courses is on the right rear of the car and the driver's side tires are changed first. The Robert Yates crew worked this stop during the 1996 exhibition race in Suzuka, Japan.

Radio headset

Rear-tire changer

One-pump jack

Tire carriers

143

Inside the Car

THE COCKPIT OF a stock car is the driver's office. Much of the interior is designed to keep drivers comfortable at speeds to 200 mph and racing temperatures in excess of 120 degrees. Everything is measured to fit the driver, from the height and travel of the foot pedals to the angle of the seat to the positioning of the steering wheel. Some drivers like to have the dashboard gauges rotated so the needle of each gauge faces directly up when the car is operating at peak efficiency. This way, one glance is all the driver needs to monitor the systems. For the driver, the most critical part of the cockpit is the seat and its five-point belting system. Just behind the seat is the water tank reservoir for the driver's cooling system.

▲ GROUND EFFECTS

Stock cars tend to fly when air gets under the front end during a high-speed crash. When the front wheels lose contact with the track, roof flaps are triggered to force the car back onto the surface.

◀ THE FAMILY SEDAN

The interior of early racing stock cars differed very little from the stock passenger car of the day.

◀ EARLY INNOVATIONS

By the early 1960s, interiors were developed to enhance safety and driver comfort as the speeds and distances of races increased.

◀ SINGULAR PURPOSE

The cockpit of a Pro Stock drag racer is vastly different from a Winston Cup car. Engine gauges are off to the right. Drivers watch the track and the large tachometer in front of them.

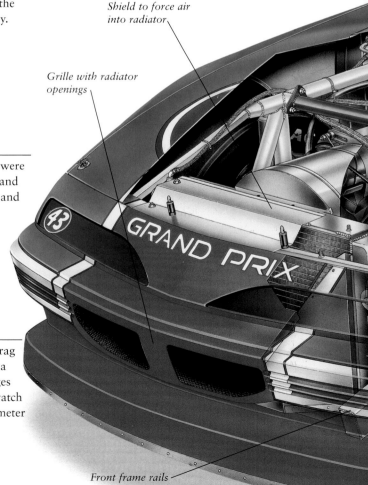

Shield to force air into radiator

Grille with radiator openings

Front frame rails

◀ENERGY SOURCE

The fuel cell is in the trunk inside its own roll cage. The large tube at left is for refueling. The plastic hose is the vent that empties excess fuel from the cell.

Roll cage

Driver cooling system vent

Refueling tube

4-barrel carburetor

Brake assembly

Side frame rails

Protective bars in driver's door

15-inch wheels with 9.5-inch rim width

Steering box

◀THE WINSTON CUP CAR

NASCAR has strict rules for its Winston Cup Series. Minimum weight is 3,300 pounds (weights in the frame rails are used to meet requirements). The V8 engines can be bored to a maximum of 358 cubic inches.

1990-2000 From T-Bird to Taurus

IN JANUARY 1997, Ford discontinued the sleek Thunderbird, which had become one of the top-performing models in the history of the NASCAR Winston Cup Series. Ford didn't have another two-door sedan that met Winston Cup specifications, so the factory quickly decided to develop the four-door Taurus, America's most popular family sedan, as its next Winston Cup car. The new Winston Cup Taurus was unveiled in 1997. Little more than a year after the idea was launched, Rusty Wallace drove the new Ford Taurus to victory lane in the Bud Shootout at Daytona International Speedway. The Taurus won 15 races in its first full season. For the 2000 season the design was upgraded with more aerodynamic fairing.

▲ TAURUSES TANGLE

Twenty drivers drove the new Ford Taurus in the 1998 NASCAR Winston Cup season. Included were Mark Martin (No. 6), who finished second in points, Ricky Rudd (in the Tide car), and Kenny Irwin (behind Rudd).

Quick-release safety hood pins

▼ FLYING FORD

Both the Thunderbird and Taurus are strong road racing cars. Mark Martin won three times in a Thunderbird and placed second at Sears Point in a Taurus in 1999.

Functional air vent

Tommy Gale's 1983 Thunderbird was exemplary of the model that was retired in 1997 with 184 wins.

FORD TAURUS HIGHLIGHTS

December 1997 First extensive racing tests at Homestead, Florida.

February 1998 Rusty Wallace's Taurus wins Bud Shootout at Daytona International Speedway.

March 1998 Mark Martin scores first Taurus win at Las Vegas, Nevada.

September 1998 Jeff Burton scores tenth win in Taurus at Richmond, Virginia.

August 1999 Dale Jarrett scores 25th win in Taurus in Brickyard 400 at Indianapolis, Indiana.

March 6, 2000 Jeff Burton scores 500th Winston Cup Ford win in a Taurus at Las Vegas, Nevada.

Windshield reinforcements

Driver safety cage

Driver's window net

Display number for 2000 Taurus introduction

15-inch racing wheels

▲ UPDATED TAURUS

Although the Ford Taurus design was only two years old, Ford improved the already advanced aerodynamic properties of the body for the 2000 season.

147

1990-2000 Modern Dirt Tracks

THE OLDEST ESTABLISHED stock car organization in the United States is not NASCAR. That honor goes to the Iowa-based International Motor Contest Association, which was established in 1915. Back then, all of the IMCA's races were run on dirt ovals. And dirt tracks still host most of the IMCA schedule. Most popular among its five divisions are the Modified, Stock, and Hobby Stock classes. The modified division has campaigned since 1979. There, the driver's quest for speed and power is tempered by a rule that allows opponents to claim the engine for $375. The IMCA sanctions races in 23 states from coast to coast, although the majority of its circuits are in the Midwest. The IMCA represents stock car racing in its purest grassroots form – Saturday night events run on rural tracks.

▲ CEREMONIAL PARADE

The entrants in September's annual IMCA Supernationals on the third-mile dirt oval at Iowa's Boone Speedway salute the crowd with a ceremonial, four-abreast parade lap before the start.

◀ STRICTLY STOCK

Jeff McMeekin of Laurel, Iowa, ran a Chevrolet Monte Carlo in the basic stock car class.

No glass windshield

"Nerf" bar for bumping

Unprotected front wheel

Exhaust system

► THE ART OF SLIDING

Bert McDaniel turned right to
keep control while sliding his
Buick through a turn on Iowa's
Marshalltown Speedway.

▼ HIGHLY MODIFIED

Wayne Graybeal (No. 101) of
Springfield, Missouri, drove inside
Rex Merritt of Billings, Missouri,
in a Modified Division race.

Driver's safety net

Lowered roofline

No rear spoiler

Treaded tires

1990-2000 Dodge Races Back

THE CHRYSLER 300s of the 1950s were the most powerful and successful stock cars of the era. Petty Enterprises' association with Chrysler, Dodge, and Plymouth resulted in eight NASCAR championships – two for Lee and six for Richard. But Chrysler began a retreat from stock car racing shortly thereafter. The factory association ended with the Pettys' switch to General Motors in 1979. In 1999 Chrysler announced it would return to the Winston Cup circuit beginning with the Daytona 500 of 2001. Named to head the development of the new Dodge Intrepid race car was Ray Evernham, one of racing's top innovators while crew chief for three-time champion Jeff Gordon. Dodge gave Evernham 500 days to get the Intrepid from concept to the track.

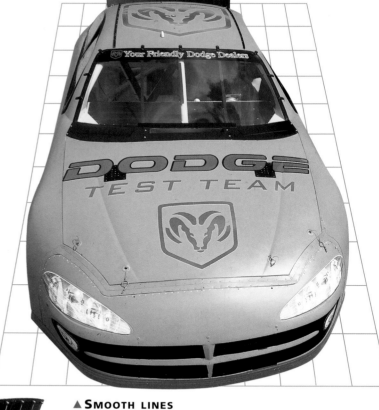

▲ SMOOTH LINES

Before building a full-sized Intrepid, Evernham's design team built a 3/8th-scale model to be used in wind tunnel testing.

◄ DODGE GURU

Ray Evernham was not only given the task of developing the Dodge Intrepid for NASCAR Winston Cup racing, he became the owner of a two-car team.

Dodge insignia

Distinctive Dodge grille

DODGE RACING HIGHLIGHTS

NASCAR Winston Cup Titles

Year	Driver	Make
1954	Lee Petty	Chrysler
1955	Tim Flock	Chrysler
1956	Buck Baker	Chrysler
1959	Lee Petty	Plymouth
1964	Richard Petty	Plymouth
1966	David Pearson	Dodge
1967	Richard Petty	Plymouth
1970	Bobby Isaac	Dodge
1971	Richard Petty	Plymouth
1972	Richard Petty	Plymouth
1974	Richard Petty	Dodge
1975	Richard Petty	Dodge

▶ FIRST TESTS

Kyle Petty drove the first on-track tests of the Dodge Intrepid in May, 2000 on the 1.5-mile oval at Florida's Homestead-Miami Speedway. The car tested was the fourth prototype developed.

▼ BUILDING A TEAM

Dodge had no problem finding teams to run the Intrepid when it returned to NASCAR Winston Cup racing. Within nine months of the announcement, four teams signed on to run seven Intrepids.

Radio antenna

Roof rail

1990-2000 2000 and Beyond

No American sport charged into the millennium with more momentum than stock car racing. The National Hot Rod Association saw more entries in its stock car-based Funny Car and Pro Stock divisions while the Pro Stock Truck class continued to grow. Trans-Am got a boost from the introduction of the Jaguar and DiTomaso Mangusta to line up alongside Ford Mustangs and Chevrolet Camaros and Corvettes. The NASCAR-backed Grand American Series entered the picture as competition for the American Le Mans Series. Off-road racing marked the year with two extreme endurance tests, the Nevada 2000 and the SCORE Baja 2000. But NASCAR led the way again with its Winston Cup Series. Just weeks into 2000, NASCAR signed the richest television contract yet awarded a motorsport organization.

▲ RICH HERITAGE

Chrysler's return to NASCAR racing restores a legendary name to the sport. After winning 12 Winston Cup championships the factory withdrew from racing, with the last of 311 wins scored by Neil Bonnett in a Dodge in 1977.

Main sponsor

▼ THE NEW BREED

Joe Gibbs expanded his Pontiac team in 1999 to create an opening for Tony Stewart, who won three races and was the Winston Cup Rookie of the Year.

► **EARNHARDT, CONTINUED**

After two straight NASCAR Busch Grand National Series championships, Dale Earnhardt Jr. moved to the Winston Cup in 2000 and scored his first victory at Texas Motor Speedway in his 12th career start.

Exhaust pipes

▲ **YOUNG CHARGER**

The Wood brothers tabbed 25-year-old Rookie of the Year candidate Elliott Sadler to run their Ford Taurus in the 2000 season.

RACING PERSONALITIES

The emergence of stock car racing as a major player on the American sports scene is more than just a story of auto races. It is one of dreamers and schemers; owners and mechanics, as well as drivers – the men who molded the sport and with it the cars of their day. Yes, drivers are center stage. From such pioneers as Red Byron, Herb Thomas, and Lee Petty, through legendary drivers the like of Richard Petty, David Pearson, and Cale Yarborough, to modern-era greats such as Dale Earnhardt and Jeff Gordon, NASCAR's Winston Cup superstars have dominated the public's attention. But the feats of other drivers, such as Trans-Am champs Mark Donohue and Tommy Kendall and USAC champ Don White, rank high in the sport as well. And this is also the story of men who promoted stock car racing, turned wrenches, set rules and standards, and spread the word. The story of stock car racing is as much one of men as of machines.

A

BOBBY ALLISON
1937–

The most successful member of the famed Alabama Gang, Bobby Allison was both a hard-nosed competitor and friendly ambassador as stock car racing began drawing more national attention in the 1970s. Although he is tied for third on the all-time Winston Cup victory list with 84 wins, Allison often raced at out-of-the-way tracks on off weekends to spread the word about stock car racing. He was voted national Driver of the Year in 1972 for winning ten races and taking 11 poles (including a record 5 straight) and again in 1983 when he claimed his only Winston Cup title. His 50 superspeedway victories included three wins in the Daytona 500, the last of which came in 1988 when he led son Davey to the checkered flag. He was voted NASCAR's Most Popular Driver six times.

BOBBY ALLISON

Only Richard Petty led more races than Bobby Allison, who won NASCAR Modified championships in 1964 and 1965 before turning to Winston Cup stock cars.

DAVEY ALLISON

DAVEY ALLISON
1961–1993

In 1987, Bobby Allison's son, Davey, became the first rookie ever to qualify for the front row of the Daytona 500. A year later he finished second to his father in the race. Davey won five races in both the 1991 and 1992 seasons and finished third in points both years. He won 19 of his 191 Winston Cup starts including the 1992 Daytona 500. Tragically, he died in a helicopter accident at Talladega Superspeedway on July 15, 1993. At the time of the accident he led the tour in points and appeared headed for his first Winston Cup title.

BUCK BAKER

B

BUCK BAKER
1919–

The first two-time champion of what became NASCAR's premier Winston Cup series, Elzie Wylie Baker is among the more versatile drivers ever to climb behind the wheel of a stock car. In 1939, Baker was driving a bus in his native Charlotte, North Carolina, when he decided to try his hand at racing. He won the 1956 Winston Cup title (and 14 races) in a Carl Kiekhaefer-owned Dodge. By the time he retired after the 1976 Firecracker 400 at Daytona International Speedway, Baker had won races in NASCAR's Modified, Speedway (IndyCars), Grand American, and Winston Cup divisions. Baker went out on his own in 1957 and repeated to give Chevrolet its first title. He ranks 13th all-time with 13 Winston Cup wins. He is ninth in poles (44) and tenth in starts (631).

BUDDY BAKER
1941–

His fellow drivers referred to Buddy Baker as "Bigfoot." It was a tribute, because few drivers were ever able to coax more speed from a car than Buck Baker's son. In March, 1970, at Alabama's Talladega Superspeedway, Buddy became the first stock car driver to break the 200-mph barrier, circling the 2 ½-mile high-banked oval at 200.447 mph in a winged Dodge Daytona. In 1980, Baker averaged 177.602 in an Oldsmobile Cutlass to win the fastest Daytona 500 ever run. Six of his 19 career wins and seven of his poles came on the famed high-banked superspeedways of Daytona and Talladega. Baker ranks tenth on NASCAR's all-time list with 40 poles. Upon retiring as a driver in 1994, Baker became a television commentator.

BUDDY BAKER

GEOFF BODINE
1949–

The oldest of the three Bodine brothers to reach the NASCAR Winston Cup tour, Geoff Bodine worked his way up from his Chemung, New York, base. From racing micro-midgets at the age of six, Geoff moved first to NASCAR's Modified Division, then to the NASCAR Busch Grand National Series before being named the NASCAR Winston Cup Rookie of the Year in 1982. Bodine scored his first three Winston Cup wins in 1984 while driving for rookie car owner Rick Hendrick. The winner of the 1986 Daytona 500, Bodine also drove for such famed owners as Junior Johnson and Bud Moore before buying the team of the late Alan Kulwicki in 1993 to realize his dream of being an owner-driver. After winning four races, he closed his shop in 1997. Bodine's brothers, Todd and Brett, also raced on the Winston Cup tour.

NEIL BONNETT

NEIL BONNETT
1946–1994

A member of the Alabama Gang and a close friend of Dale Earnhardt, Neil Bonnett was extremely popular with fans and fellow drivers. Born in Bessemer, Alabama, Bonnett followed the leads of Red Farmer and brothers Bobby and Donnie Allison. Fast and smooth, Bonnett gained rides with some of NASCAR's top owners, including the Wood brothers and Junior Johnson. He won back-to-back Coca-Cola 600s at Charlotte, North Carolina, in 1982–83 driving for the Wood brothers. Half of his career 18 wins were with the Wood brothers.

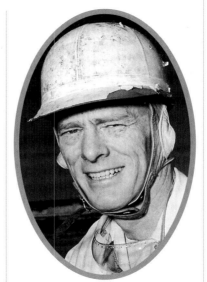

RED BYRON

RED BYRON
1915–1960

The role that Red Byron played in the launching of NASCAR cannot be underestimated. A tail gunner on a bomber in the Pacific theater during World War II, Byron built and raced cars out of his Atlanta garage when the Georgia city served as the hub of stock car racing. When Bill France Sr. formed NASCAR in 1948, the respected Byron had doubts about the organization. But when he decided to back France, other drivers followed his lead. Byron won NASCAR's first title in the Modified Division in 1948 and a year later won the first NASCAR stock car championship. Due to failing health, he stopped racing in 1951. He then teamed with Briggs Cunningham in trying to develop an American sports car to challenge at the 24 Hours of Le Mans.

RICHARD CHILDRESS
1950–

As a driver, Richard Childress struggled throughout his career. His best finish in a NASCAR Winston Cup race was a third in 1978. The most he ever won as a driver was $157,530 in 1980. But Childress had an eye for talent and made his mark as a car owner through his association with driver Dale Earnhardt. Together, Earnhardt and Childress have won 65 races and six Winston Cup races since joining forces in 1984 with sponsors Chevrolet and GM Goodwrench Service.

GEOFF BODINE

RICHARD CHILDRESS

D

ERNIE DERR
1929–

The best-known organization in stock car racing is NASCAR, but there are a number of other series out there. And starting in 1951, Ernie Derr visited and won titles in most of them: IMCA, ARCA, MARC, and others too numerous to mention. A manager of an auto parts store in Keokuk, Iowa, Derr was a one-man racing operation. He owned, prepared, and drove

ERNIE DERR

his own cars – most notably a line of Dodge Chargers in the 1960s and 1970s that carried him to many of his estimated 350 wins and 12 national championships. Derr was equally at home on dirt and asphalt, as well as behind a typewriter. On top of all the things he accomplished as a race car driver, Ernie Derr was also his own publicist.

JUNIE DONLAVEY
1924–

Just after World War II, Junie Donlavey fancied himself a race car driver. Then reality hit: he just wasn't very good. So Donlavey turned to preparing and owning cars for other drivers, launching a career that has spanned seven decades. The first car he owned was driven in NASCAR's Modified division in 1949. Donlavey entered a car in the first Southern 500 in 1950 with Bob Apperson driving and Runt Harris in relief. He is the only active Winston Cup owner on the tour who had a car in the 1950 Southern 500. His cars have started nearly 800 NASCAR Winston Cup races.

JUNIE DONLAVEY

His forte is working with young drivers and he has fielded three Rookies of the Year – Bill Dennis (1970), Jody Ridley (1980), and Ken Schrader (1985). Junie's only victory came with Ridley driving in the 1981 Mason-Dixon 500 at Dover, Delaware.

MARK DONOHUE
1937–1975

One of the most gifted drivers and road racers of his era, Mark Donohue won stock car

MARK DONOHUE

races on both the Trans-Am and NASCAR Winston Cup circuits. But he wasn't just a stock car racer. Donohue graduated from Brown University with a degree in engineering. His first motor competition was a hill climb in 1959 that he won with a Corvette. Six years later, Donohue drew his first attention as the Sports Car Club of America's Driver of the Year for winning two national championships. But it was the launching of the factory-driven Trans-Am "pony car" in the mid-1960s that also sent Donohue's career skyrocketing. Driving Chevrolet Camaros and AMC Javelins, Donohue came within ten points of winning five straight Trans-Am titles. His record of 29 race wins still stands. In 1972, Donohue won the Indianapolis 500. In 1973, he won the NASCAR race on the road course at Riverside, California, to give the AMC Matador model its first Winston Cup victory. He won races in both the US Road Racing Championships and the Can-Am Series and eventually made his way to the world-championship Formula One

circuit, where he died on August 19, 1975, of injuries suffered while practicing for the Austrian Grand Prix.

E

CLAY EARLES
1913–1999

The grandson of a Civil War veteran, Clay Earles liked to refer to his birthplace as "L.A." That would be Lower Axton, Virginia, and the site was his parents' struggling tobacco farm. Earles took his first job at the age of ten and eventually began dabbling in real estate when he came into possession of a dirt race track in his home of Martinsville, Virginia. After spending several lean years promoting car thrill shows and jalopy races, Earles signed an agreement with Bill France Sr. to host a NASCAR Strictly Stock race at Martinsville in 1949. Earles shared France's dream for NASCAR, although he lost money on every NASCAR event he promoted for the first five years. In 1954 he made just enough profit to pave the .526-mile oval. In 1956, Martinsville played host

CLAY EARLES

DALE EARNHARDT

CHRIS ECONOMAKI

BILL ELLIOTT
1955–

Bill Elliott has never wandered from his roots of Dawsonville, Georgia. In fact, his nickname became "Awesome Bill from Dawsonville." Perennially voted NASCAR's Most Popular Driver by the fans, Elliott charged into NASCAR racing with a flair that reminded many fans of the legends who preceded him. Elliott's 1985 season remains one of the greatest in Winston Cup history and helped the sport soar to new heights. Elliott won 11 races and 11 poles, all on superspeedways. He also won three of NASCAR's four majors: the Daytona 500, the Winston 500 at Talladega, and the Southern 500 at Darlington. He also won NASCAR's Winston Million the first time it was offered, and he won the Winston Cup title in 1988. Elliott's 40 career wins and 49 poles have all come in Fords, making him second (behind David Pearson) in wins for that factory. He holds the fastest qualifying record in NASCAR history: 212.809 mph, at Talladega in 1987.

to NASCAR's first 500-lap race. To this day, NASCAR hosts two races a year on its senior track.

DALE EARNHARDT
1951–

Dubbed "The Intimidator," Dale Earnhardt was the top driver on the NASCAR Winston Cup circuit as the sport began its rapid growth in the late 1980s and early 1990s. The son of the late Ralph Earnhardt, who won 250 short-track races and NASCAR's 1956 Sportsman Division championship, Dale claimed his seventh NASCAR Winston Cup title in 1994 to tie Richard Petty for the most titles won. Earnhardt won his first title in 1980 while driving for Rod Osterlund. The next six (1986, '87, '90, '91, '93, and '94) came while he drove Chevrolets owned by Richard Childress. Earnhardt was twice honored as the American Driver of the Year (1987 and '94) and won three International Race of

Champions titles (1990, '95, and '99). From 1990 through 1999, Earnhardt won ten straight Twin 125 qualifying races at Daytona International Speedway. He won the Daytona 500 in 1998. Earnhardt ranks sixth in career Winston Cup wins and finished the century as NASCAR's all-time leading money winner.

CHRIS ECONOMAKI
1920–

Born in Brooklyn, New York, racing fan Chris Economaki got his first taste of car racing at age seven on a board track at Atlantic City, New Jersey. The sport that Economaki discovered that day was one that he would introduce to millions of Americans in the 1960s and 1970s as an expert television commentator. A print journalist by trade, he remains at the helm of the respected National Speed Sports News. Economaki first branched out as a track announcer. When television

networks began covering races, they needed someone in the pits to tell viewers what was happening. The right man for that job was Economaki, whose reports from Indianapolis to Daytona and beyond helped spread the word.

BILL ELLIOTT

RICHIE EVANS

RICHIE EVANS
1941–1985

Richie Evans didn't drive the standard stock car, but he has one of stock car racing's top win totals. His forte was the Modified, a hybrid stock car souped up for short tracks. Racing out of his Rome, New York, hometown, Evans won more than 500 races in his career. He also won nine NASCAR Modified Division season championships, including eight straight from 1978–85. He won 37 races in the 1979 season and finished in the top five in 54 of his 60 starts. Richie Evans became known to fans as NASCAR's "King of Modifieds."

RAY EVERNHAM
1957–

He wanted to be a driver and made his first start in a Modified at age 14. But by the time he was 24, Ray Evernham saw that his real talent was outside the car, not in it. So he stopped driving and became one of the most influential behind-the-scenes forces in stock car history, first as car manager for the International Race of Champions from

1984–89 then as crew chief for Jeff Gordon. When Chrysler decided to return to NASCAR Winston Cup racing for the 2001 season, Evernham was their choice to develop the car. But it was as the mechanical and strategical guru for Gordon's meteoric rise that Evernham earned national

RAY EVERNHAM

recognition in the last decade of the 20th century. Evernham was Gordon's crew chief when the then 19-year-old driver made his NASCAR Busch Grand National debut in 1990. When Rick Hendrick signed Gordon as a driver in 1992, he

signed Evernham as the crew chief. Evernham and Gordon were together for 216 races. Gordon won 47 of those and the NASCAR Winston Cup titles in 1995, 1997, and 1998. Not only did Evernham know cars, he knew his driver. On the radio during races, Evernham was a calming, settling voice who was usually a step ahead of the opposition in race strategy. Evernham was also responsible for the Rainbow Warriors pit crew and the shop team that gave Gordon cars that finished in all but 18 of their last 154 races together. Evernham remained with the Hendrick racing team until late in the 1999 season.

RED FARMER
1932–

The patriarch of NASCAR's Alabama Gang, Farmer stakes claim to being the winningest driver in stock car history, although even he has lost

count of his main-event triumphs. The number tops 700 in a career that spanned five decades. Farmer won NASCAR's Modified title in 1956 and three consecutive NASCAR Busch Series, Grand National Division championships from 1969–71. Farmer spent most of his racing career on the short track circuit and made only 36 starts at the Winston Cup level, with his best result being a fourth place finish.

HERB FISHEL
1941–

If ever a man was born to be a part of racing, it was Herb Fishel. He was raised in Winston-Salem, North Carolina, near the heart of southern stock car racing, and earned a degree in mechanical engineering from North Carolina State University. That degree took him to Detroit in 1963 to join the Chevrolet Drafting Department. Six years later, Fishel was transferred to the Chevrolet

RED FARMER

Product Performance Group and was working on racing programs alongside the likes of childhood heroes Junior Johnson and Smokey Yunick. In 1976, Fishel became manager of Buick's Special Products Engineering Group and was responsible for the development of the Regals that won three straight NASCAR Winston Cup titles (1981–83). By then he had returned to Chevrolet to head a program that developed into the Chevrolet Raceshop. In 1991 General Motors decided to put all its racing activities under one roof in a division called GM Racing. The man named to head the organization was Fishel. He was a logical and deserving choice. Under Fishel, GM's achievements include nine straight NASCAR Winston Cup Manufacturers Championships (1983–91) and nine victories in 12 years in the Daytona 500, six consecutive Indianapolis 500 wins from 1988 to 1993 with the Chevy Indy V8, and three more with the Oldsmobile Aurora V8 from 1997 to 1999. He also won victories in other such diversified racing events as the 24 Hours of Daytona, the 12 Hours of Sebring, sports endurance races, and the SCORE Baja 1000 race.

FONTY FLOCK
1921–1972

Truman Fontell Flock never denied that his racing roots grew in the moonshine trade. He learned to drive at age 12 so that he could serve as lookout for his older brother Carl and an uncle in their moonshine business. Several years later, Fonty was making two runs a day between Atlanta and Dawsonville, Georgia. His legal racing career began because Atlanta was the hub of Modified racing as well as moonshining. After serving in the US Army Air Corps in World War II, he took racing more seriously. He was the uncrowned king of Modifieds in 1947 and won the NASCAR Modified title two years later. From there, he went on to what would later become known as the NASCAR Winston Cup Series where his success continued, as he won 19 of his 154 starts.

FONTY FLOCK

TIM FLOCK
1924–1998

Before the Pettys, the Flocks were the first family of stock car racing. Tim, Fonty, and Bob raced stock cars, as did sister Ethel. Senior brother Carl raced boats. Tim was the youngest of the brothers and the most successful driver in the family. But although Tim became NASCAR's second two-time champion, perhaps

TIM FLOCK

his greatest claim to fame was Jocko, the pet monkey who rode as Flock's co-pilot early in his career. Flock won his first title in 1952 driving a boxy Hudson Hornet. Three years later, he won his second title in the powerful Chrysler 300 owned by Carl Kiekhaefer. Flock's 18 wins and 19 poles in 1955 were NASCAR Winston Cup records. The pole record still stands; the win record stood until Richard Petty won 27 races in 1967. Flock won 21.2 percent of his career starts (40 for 189) and finished in the top five 55 percent of the time.

GEORGE FOLLMER
1934–

A Southern California insurance salesman by trade, George Follmer came late to racing. His first competition was a rally at the age of 25, and he didn't compete in a national series until he was 30. But at the age of 39, Follmer won a world championship point in his first Formula One race – scoring yet another milestone in a career that ripened with age. Follmer first gained recognition in 1964 as the U.S. Road Racing Championships season winner in the under-2-liter class. After two more seasons on the USRRC and Can-Am circuits, with side trips to the 24 Hours of Le Mans, Follmer joined the Trans-Am Series in 1968 as a factory driver for AMC Javelin. He finished a distant second on points behind Mark Donohue. His big break came in 1969 after he won an IndyCar race by three laps at Phoenix International Raceway using a stock-block Chevy V8 engine. Bud Moore signed Follmer as the No. 2 driver behind Parnelli Jones on his Trans-Am team of Ford Mustangs. He finished seventh in points in 1969 and third in 1970, winning one race each year. In 1971, he won three races and finished second five times in his ten starts, but still finished second in points. Follmer returned to Javelin in 1972, and won four races and the Trans-Am championship.

GEORGE FOLLMER

JIM FOSTER
1927–

Although he was raised just down the street from stock car racing's legendary Bowman-Gray Stadium in Winston-Salem, North Carolina, Jim Foster had no interest in racing as a youth. He loved the traditional sports and after serving in the Navy in World War II, became assistant sports editor of the *Greensboro (North Carolina) Record*. To balance the paper's coverage, he started a motorsports column. From that point, both media coverage of stock car

JIM FOSTER

racing and Foster's role in the sport expanded. Foster helped organize the Southern Motorsports Writers Association and Stock Car Racing Hall of Fame. After spreading the word as a writer and sports editor, Foster went on to become one of the leading public relations personnel in stock car racing.

A. J. FOYT
1935–

Although he is far better known for his exploits in open-wheel cars, four-time Indy 500 champion Anthony Joseph Foyt raced in both the NASCAR Winston Cup and US Auto Club stock car series when possible. Foyt won the Daytona 500 in 1972 to join

A. J. FOYT

Mario Andretti as the only drivers to win both the Indy 500 and Daytona 500. Foyt also was a two-time winner of the 24 Hours of Daytona sports car endurance race. Foyt won seven Winston Cup races in 128 starts. Over the 1971 and 1972 seasons, Foyt had four wins, five poles, and nine top-five finishes in 13 starts in the Wood Brothers Mercury. Foyt's last stock car start came in the inaugural Brickyard 400 in 1994 at his beloved Indianapolis Motor Speedway.

BILL FRANCE
1911–1992

Born in tiny Horse Pasture, Virginia, and raised in Washington, DC, William Henry Getty France painted houses and owned a garage to make money to raise a family, race cars, and promote races shortly after World War II. But it was in his role as NASCAR's benevolent dictator that France made his mark. A man of stature and vision, the six-foot-five France built one of the most powerful organizations in racing. France's National Association for Stock Car Auto Racing was founded in 1948 to protect drivers, owners, and fans from ruthless and unethical promoters. Under France's direction, stock car racing expanded from its regional southern roots to a national sport. France's "Strictly Stock" series of 1949 grew into the Winston Cup. He built Daytona International Speedway and conceived the idea of Speed Weeks. Not only did he build NASCAR; he worked tirelessly to guarantee competitive balance – fending off repeated challenges from rival racing organizations, manufacturers, and drivers.

BILL "BIG BILL" FRANCE

BILL FRANCE, JR

BILL FRANCE JR.
1932–

Although not technically a Junior, William Clifton France took his father's vision and ran with it, expanding NASCAR from its southern base into a national sports organization. Starting with the adoption of the streamlined schedule of the Winston Cup Series for its premier division in 1972, NASCAR gained national television exposure and entered eight new markets in the west and north during Bill France Jr.'s tenure as president. France developed NASCAR from a family-run operation to an international corporation. In 1979, the first live telecast of the Daytona 500 opened the door for live television coverage of every race. France stepped down as NASCAR president at the end of the 1998 season but remains CEO for the International Speedway Corporation.

NORRIS FRIEL
1906–1972

When Bill France Sr. formed NASCAR, he promised a level playing field for all competitors. As chief of NASCAR's technical team, Norris Friel became the man who enforced and helped write the rules during the formative years. A friend of France's from their days in Washington, D.C., Friel developed his technical expertise from 20 years as a car agency service manager and 16 years on the AAA Contest Board. France hired Friel when AAA quit racing and NASCAR was dealing with the controversial post-race

NORRIS FRIEL

disqualifications of race winners Tim Flock and Fireball Roberts. Although Friel's technical staff was mainly concerned with equalizing engine rules, his administration also initiated safety changes.

G

HARRY GANT
1940–

Although he was late coming into the NASCAR Winston Cup Series, Harry Gant was a

HARRY GANT

Winston Cup rookie at age 39 following a successful short-track career. Gant won 18 Winston Cup races and finished second in the series in 1984. Gant had time to twice add his name to the record book before retiring in 1994. In 1991 he tied a modern era record with four straight wins starting with the Southern 500 at Darlington. He also won two Busch Grand National races during the run. Almost a year later, Gant eclipsed Bobby Allison to become the oldest driver ever to win a Winston Cup race when he triumphed at Michigan at the age of 52.

BOB GLIDDEN
1944–

A former line mechanic at a Ford dealership in Whiteland, Indiana, Bob Glidden brought national attention to Pro Stock drag racing over a 25-year run that began in 1972. Glidden set National Hot Rod Association records for most professional wins with 85 and

national championships, with ten, all in the Pro Stock class. Glidden launched his drag racing career in modified Fords in NHRA's Stock and Super Stock divisions. Only four times in his career did Glidden go an entire season without a victory, and his five consecutive championships from 1985 to 1989 became an NHRA record. Glidden is a member of the Motorsports Hall of Fame.

BOB GLIDDEN

ELI GOLD
1953–

Born and raised in Brooklyn, New York, Gold has one of the most recognizable voices in NASCAR racing. In 1976, he joined the Motor Racing Network radio team and became the network's co-anchor for broadcasts of NASCAR events. He moved on to the Nashville Network's television broadcasts, anchoring many NASCAR events. He has been the host of NASCAR Live, a weekly radio show featuring racing guests and interviews, for more than a decade.

JEFF GORDON
1971–

The Boy Wonder of NASCAR Winston Cup racing, Gordon first climbed into a go-kart at the age of three and started racing at five in a quarter-midget. Because California law prevented Gordon from racing professionally until the age of 16, his family moved to Indiana to advance his career. He became the youngest driver ever to win a USAC national title when he won the midget title at age 18. A year later, he doubled as USAC's Silver Crown champion and the Rookie of the Year in the NASCAR Busch Grand National Series. Gordon became the second-youngest driver ever to win a NASCAR Winston Cup title in 1995 at the age of 24. He followed that success with two more titles (1997–98) and led the Winston Cup series in wins for five straight years (1995–99). By the end of the millennium, Gordon's winning record of 22 percent was the highest in history, and he was still more than a year shy of his 30th birthday.

JEFF GORDON

H

BARNEY HALL
1934–

Long before stock car racing made it to national television, the voice of Barney Hall drifted across the southern landscape on sunny Sunday afternoons like a cooling

BARNEY HALL

summer breeze. Hall brought his insider's view of the NASCAR Winston Cup action to scattered fans across the south – and beyond, as the sport grew – via radio as the lead announcer for the Motor Racing Network in its early years. Hall's distinctive delivery made him nearly as recognizable as the drivers he covered. And he had almost as many fans. Hall knew his sport. He also knew the sport's drivers, and he wove this knowledge into his broadcasts, some of which extended more than four hours. When President Carter invited a group of NASCAR drivers to visit the White House, they invited Barney Hall to go along for the historic ride. He did – and told the world about

it as though it were just another of the steps in NASCAR's rise, which it certainly was.

ROY HALL
1921–1992

"Rapid" Roy Hall had a theory on life: "When it's time to go, I'll go. Until then, I have nothing to lose." And that's how he lived his life – which included both sanctioned and clandestine racing. When Hall arrived in Daytona Beach, Florida, for the 1940 race, he already had a reputation. More than one source had pronounced Hall the "national" champion for 1939, when he was 18, for his famed exploits at the Lakewood Speedway outside of Atlanta, Georgia. But it was another type of racing, whiskey running, that was fueling Hall's double-edged reputation of being a skilled if reckless driver. Hall claimed that he had averaged 62 mph in his 1939 Ford

ROY HALL

Coupe just to get to Daytona Beach. Then he won with a record average speed of 76.53 mph. And he won again in 1941. On the track, Hall had

the services of car owner Raymond Parks and famed mechanic Red Vogt. But he twice did time for moonshine running and, in 1946, was jailed for two years for robbery. Shortly after being released from prison in 1949, Hall suffered major head injuries at Tri-Point Speedway in High Point, North Carolina, and raced infrequently thereafter.

RAY HENDRICK

RAY HENDRICK
1929–1990

His base was Richmond, Virginia, but Ray Hendrick was seldom home. Hendrick was a racer who ran anywhere and everywhere over a 29-year career. Wins meant a lot to Hendrick. He won as many as 712 main events, but he never won a NASCAR season championship. Why? Because Hendrick paid little attention to the series. But he would race four and five times a week, sometimes twice on the same day. His forte was Modifieds and the Late Model Sportsman. But Hendrick got just as much excitement from running at a local track as he did from a NASCAR touring race, which made him a folk

hero at small tracks around the Virginias. At one time Hendrick held the record for wins at Martinsville, Virginia. How good was Hendrick? He made 17 NASCAR Winston Cup Series starts and had two top-five and six top-ten finishes. He could run with the big boys. Most of the time, he just chose not to.

RICK HENDRICK
1949–

Ever since becoming the youngest Chevrolet dealer in America when he opened a car lot at the age of 23 in Bentsville, South Carolina, Rick Hendrick has been building. Today, the Hendrick Automotive Group controls 84 car and truck dealerships in 65 locations across the United States. But it is as the chief executive officer of Hendrick Motorsports that Hendrick is best known. He got his start in racing in 1980 in the dangerous sport of boat drag racing. He won three national championships and his boat Nitro Fever set a world record of 222.2 mph in 1982. He got into NASCAR Winston

RICK HENDRICK

Cup racing in 1984 with Geoff Bodine as his driver. Bodine won three races and finished ninth in the standings, and Hendrick was off to the races. He fielded two cars in 1986 and at times ran four in 1987. He has usually campaigned three a season since, even when he was in a two-year battle with cancer. From 1995–99, Hendrick's drivers won four NASCAR Winston Cup titles – Jeff Gordon three (1995, 1997, 1998) and Terry Labonte one (1996) – and 55 races.

JOHN HOLMAN

JOHN HOLMAN AND RALPH MOODY
1917–1978 AND 1918–

The unlikely partners converted Ford's withdrawal from stock car racing in 1957 into one of the most powerful teams in the history of racing. The stocky John Holman was a gregarious man who was raised in California after being born in Nashville, Tennessee. He got his start in business by buying salvage in Texas and selling it in California, using the time it

took his checks to clear to race his goods across the Southwest to market. He got his start in racing in the early 1950s supplying parts to Lincolns in the Pan-American road races. Ralph Moody was born and raised in Massachusetts, where he raced midgets before World War II and operated several high-performance shops. The quiet Moody was also one of NASCAR's more respected early drivers. Both men were working for the Ford team in 1957 when the factory decided

RALPH MOODY

to get out of racing. Holman and Moody got a loan, bought the entire Ford operation, and started supplying other teams as well as running their own operation and taking the lead in research and development. The stable of Holman-Moody drivers included Fireball Roberts, David Pearson, and Cale Yarborough. Holman-Moody built endurance cars for the 24 Hours of Le Mans as well as stock cars. They also made high-performance boats with Ford engines. Pearson

won back-to-back NASCAR Winston Cup titles in Holman-Moody Fords in 1968 and 1969. Even after Ford officially returned to racing in 1962, Holman-Moody parts were prized until the partnership dissolved in 1971.

TOMMY HOUSTON
1945–

Born in Hickory, North Carolina, Tommy Houston got his start with automobiles by rebuilding a 1957 Ford. He started racing full time in 1972 and competed in NASCAR's Late Model Sportsman Division before it became the Busch Grand National Series. Although he never won a season championship, Houston set a record by starting the first 360 races of NASCAR's Busch Grand National Series beginning with the tour's inception in 1982. Houston is the all-time leader in Grand National starts (417), top-five finishes (123), and top-ten finishes (198), and ranks third on the all-time list of race winners with 24. At one time, he was the leader in career earnings. Houston was the first driver to win on the Busch Grand National Series in a Chevy (1982) and a Buick (1985). In 1987, he qualified at 194.389 mph at Daytona International Speedway, a record that still stands as the fastest qualifying lap in Grand National Series history.

HARRY HYDE
1926–

Some called him old-fashioned and stubborn, and at the end of his career as a crew chief, Harry Hyde saw many of his

peers wielding laptop computers rather than wrenches. But Hyde was one of the most respected crew chiefs in the history of stock car racing, with 48 victories to his credit in a career that began about the same time as NASCAR's Winston Cup. Hyde's forte was setting up cars for specific tracks. And he was at his best on the short ovals where handling is critical. "He is absolutely uncanny," veteran driver Dave Marcis once said when asked to describe Hyde's abilities. Hyde began tinkering with stock car suspensions when a majority of races were still run in the dirt, but he stayed on top of the game on asphalt. "A turn is a turn," he once said. "You can have all the power in the world, but if you can't get a car to corner, you don't have a winner." And Hyde had 48 winners in his career as a NASCAR Winston Cup crew chief. Twenty-eight of those wins and 32 of the 80 poles won by Hyde-prepared cars came with Bobby Isaac during the 1969–70 seasons. Isaac won the title in 1970 with a high-winged Dodge Daytona prepared by Hyde.

HARRY HYDE

I

JACK INGRAM
1938–

Driving in NASCAR's second-echelon series denies a driver the national spotlight, but that never bothered Jack Ingram, who made a career out of winning races in NASCAR's Late Model Sportsman and Busch Grand National series. Ingram won three straight titles (1972–74) when the secondary series was known as the Late Model Sportsman. After the tour was reorganized, Ingram won titles in 1982 and '85 under the Grand National

JACK INGRAM

banner. Ingram started 275 races and won 31, which stood as a Grand National record until it was eclipsed by Mark Martin in 1997.

DALE INMAN
1936–

Richard Petty's cousin and childhood friend Dale Inman entered racing through his association with the Petty family. Overall, Inman called the shots for cars that won 193 NASCAR Winston Cup

races. Inman grew up in Level Cross, North Carolina, just down the road from the Petty family complex. He swam in Pole Cat Creek with brothers Richard and Maurice Petty and played high school football with Richard at Randleman High. In high school, Petty was a lineman and Inman was

DALE INMAN

the star halfback. But their positions reversed when it came to racing. It was patriarch Lee Petty who got Inman into stock car racing. At first, Inman worked for Bud Moore. But he joined Richard when Petty began racing on the Winston Cup trail in 1958, when Inman, engine-building Petty brother Maurice, and The King formed the greatest family team in racing. Inman served as Petty's crew chief for 187 of his 200 victories.

BOBBY ISAAC
1932–1977

Two words were used to describe Bobby Isaac: tough and fast. Isaac dropped out of school at the age of 12 to work in a sawmill. While many of his early racing efforts on short tracks ended as boxing matches, he quickly earned a different reputation

upon joining the NASCAR Winston Cup circuit in 1964. He led every race he entered as a rookie. Isaac's 1970 season is remembered as one of the greatest single-season campaigns in NASCAR history. Driving a winged Dodge Daytona, Isaac won 11 races and 13 poles and set six track records en route to the title. In November, 1970, he turned a 201.104-mph lap at Talladega that stood as a

BOBBY ISAAC

closed-course record until it was broken in 1983. In all, Isaac won 37 Winston Cup races. He ranks sixth on the all-time list with 50 poles, including a record 20 during the 1969 season, and he led a total of 13,229 laps.

J

DALE JARRETT
1956–

A four-sport star athlete in high school in Conover, North Carolina, Dale Jarrett appeared headed toward a professional golf career when he decided to follow in his father's footsteps and take up stock car racing.

DALE JARRETT

He made his debut in 1977 at the Hickory, North Carolina, track where his dad had once promoted races. Jarrett advanced from the NASCAR Busch Grand National Series to a full-time Winston Cup ride in 1987. He won his first race with the Wood brothers in 1991 and won the first of his two Daytona 500s with Joe Gibbs in 1993. But it was after joining car owner Robert Yates in 1995 that Jarrett began to rise in the NASCAR Winston Cup standings. He claimed his first championship in 1999.

NED JARRETT
1932–

Few people have had a more positive influence on stock car racing than "Gentleman Ned" Jarrett, who won races and a title as a driver and fans as a television commentator. As a NASCAR driver, Jarrett was the second to reach 50 wins. He won the Winston Cup titles in 1961 in a Chevrolet and 1965 in a Ford. Jarrett won 14 percent of his career starts and finished in the top five 53 percent of the time. His most notable victory came in the 1965 Southern 500 when he won by 14 laps. Jarrett remains the all-time leader in wins in a Ford with 43. After retiring at the age of 35, Jarrett first turned to promoting races, then found a home behind the

NED JARRETT

microphone. It was in that second career that Jarrett expanded the family of stock car racing fans with his unique ability to make complex issues and concepts conversational.

JUNIOR JOHNSON
1931–

Robert Glenn Johnson Jr. enjoyed three brilliant stock car careers. The first was running moonshine on the back roads of North Carolina in a 1940 Ford powered by a 454-cubic-inch Cadillac engine. The second was as a NASCAR driver. Although he never ran a full schedule, Johnson won 50 races and 47 poles in a career that spanned only 313 races. Then he excelled as a car owner. Cale Yarborough and Darrell Waltrip each won three Winston Cup titles in cars owned and prepared by Johnson. A total of 38 drivers won 119 races in Johnson-

JUNIOR JOHNSON

owned cars. Johnson also became NASCAR's first literary folk hero after author Thomas Wolfe captured his life and essence in the classic essay "The Last American Hero."

WARREN JOHNSON
1943–

A General Motors enthusiast throughout his career, Warren Johnson started racing in 1963 with a '57 Chevy at bracket drag meets at Minnesota Dragway. The former engineering student at the

WARREN JOHNSON

University of Minnesota succeeded Bob Glidden as the driver to beat in the National Hot Rod Association's Pro Stock series in the early 1990s. He was also the first Pro Stock driver to exceed the 160-, 180-, 190-, and 200-mph barriers, and is the all-time NHRA leader in fast times. Johnson is third in total victories in NHRA history.

PARNELLI JONES
1933–

Nicknamed "Parnelli" by an aunt, Rufus Jones grew up in the Torrance suburb of Los Angeles, California, at a time when orange groves and dirt roads began where the subdivisions ended. He was hot-rodding by the age of 17 and flipping cars in the dirt to duplicate the feats of drivers he had seen in a stunt show. His first organized racing was in jalopies, where he was spotted by track promoter and IndyCar owner J. C. Agajanian. After winning two sprint car titles for Agajanian, Jones went to the Indianapolis 500. Jones was Rookie of the Year, won

the Indy 500 in 1963, finished second in 1965, and was leading with the controversial turbine in 1967 when it stopped running three laps from the finish. And although he later owned a series of IndyCars that won three national championships, Jones' first love was always stock cars. Jones competed on the NASCAR Winston Cup, USAC, and Trans-Am circuits and twice broke the stock car record for the Pikes Peak Hill climb driving Bill Stroppe-prepared Mercurys up the side of the Colorado mountain. Jones was a Ford lover. He won 13 USAC races and the 1964 title (he was second in 1967) in Fords. After debuting on the Trans-Am Series in 1967 in a Mercury Cougar, Jones drove Ford Mustangs for Bud Moore in 1969–70. He finished second in the championship in 1969, then won the title and five races in 1970. The last of his four Winston Cup wins came in 1967 on the road course at Riverside, California.

PARNELLI JONES

K

TOM KENDALL
1966–

A national champion while still in college at UCLA, Tom Kendall was not the typical stock car racer. Not only was hee college educated (his degree was in economics), wealthy, and tall, Kendall preferred road courses to ovals. And he turned that skill into being one of the top drivers in Trans-Am Series history and the man who headed the resurgence of Trans-Am sports sedan road racing in the 1990s. Kendall began his racing by becoming the youngest champion in the history of the defunct IMSA organization in 1986 while still a junior at UCLA. In addition to winning three IMSA GTU titles, he twice doubled as both

TOM KENDALL

the GTU and Firehawk Endurance champion. In 1990, he advanced to the Trans-Am Series and became the only four-time champion. His first Trans-Am title came in 1990 in a Chevy Beretta. He returned to Trans-Am racing in 1994 following a serious 1993 accident at Watkins Glen in a

World Sports Car. After finishing third in the 1994 Trans-Am series, he won three straight championships in a Ford Mustang Cobra, capped by a 1997 season that saw him win a record 11 straight races. Kendall is the all-time Trans-Am leader in series titles (four), fastest qualifying runs (39), and top-three finishes (53), and his 26 wins is second only to Mark Donohue's 29.

CARL KIEKHAEFER

CARL KIEKHAEFER
1906–1983

A workaholic perfectionist who was an inventor as well as an innovator, Kiekhaefer turned the principles that made him a fortune into creating one of the most powerful teams in the history of stock car racing. Raised on a farm in Mequon, Wisconsin, Kiekhaefer was a designer for Nash at the age of 19. In 1939, he paid $23,000 for a bankrupt outboard motor factory in Cedarburg, Wisconsin. He personally redesigned the engine and soon had 45,000 orders for the new Mercury outboard. During World War II he received four commendations from the government for developing some specialized military

engines. After the war, his interests turned to racing and he first raced for Ford through his connection with Mercury. But a dispute with Ford over the availability of factory parts led Kiekhaefer to switch factories and pour all his efforts into Chrysler in 1954. Early in 1955, Kiekhaefer's powerful Chryslers struggled with dirty oil, so he invented the paper oil filter that remains in use to this day. His cars won 40 races and back-to-back NASCAR Winston Cup titles in 1955 and 1956. At the pinnacle of his sport, but faced with rules designed to end his domination and challenges from Ford and General Motors, Kiekhaefer closed his shop before the 1957 season and walked away from stock car racing.

HAROLD KINDER
1928–1991

Kinder was NASCAR's flagman, its most visible official, for more than ten years, serving through the decade of the 1980s. He became the sanctioning body's seventh full-time flagman in 1980, but he had substituted frequently in the 1970s and was on the Daytona International Speedway flag stand for two of

HAROLD KINDER

Winston Cup racing's most riveting finishes, the 1976 and 1979 Daytona 500s. Kinder retired in May 1990 and died September 2, 1991. The flagstand at Lowe's Motor Speedway near Charlotte, North Carolina, is named in his honor.

ALAN KULWICKI
1954–1993

Alan Kulwicki was not the typical NASCAR Winston Cup driver. A devout Catholic from Wisconsin with a college degree in engineering, Kulwicki drove only cars that he owned and built. Even on race weekends, Kulwicki would work long into the night putting the

ALAN KULWICKI

final touches on his Ford Thunderbirds. Kulwicki was the Winston Cup Rookie of the Year in 1986 after his graduation from the mostly midwestern American Speed Association series. Then in 1992, Kulwicki won the most hotly-contested Winston Cup championship race in NASCAR history when he edged Bill Elliott by ten points. Sadly, Kulwicki was killed in a private plane crash in 1993, less than a year after winning his title.

TERRY LABONTE

TERRY LABONTE
1956–

Fewer drivers on NASCAR's Winston Cup circuit are more consistent or respected than Terry Labonte, who holds two unusual records. Labonte has made every start since 1979, and he went a record 12 seasons between his two Winston Cup championship campaigns of 1984 and 1996. Both of those title seasons were almost identical, with Labonte winning two races with 24 top-ten finishes. A rookie in the 1979 class that included Dale Earnhardt and Harry Gant, Labonte has driven for only four owners in his career – Billy Hagan, Junior Johnson, Richard Jackson, and Rick Hendrick (since 1994).

ELMO LANGLEY
1929–1997

Elmo Langley filled almost every role available in a 42-year NASCAR career that began in 1955. He was a driver, car owner, crew chief, technical official, and pace car driver. Born in Cresswell, North Carolina, but raised in Washington, D.C., by his grandparents, Langley lied about his age and joined the Navy at age 15. After leaving the service in 1946, Elmo began attending short-track races and started driving in 1952. He won four Virginia state championships and finished

ELMO LANGLEY

12th in the 1954 Southern 500 at Darlington Raceway, the first NASCAR Winston Cup race he entered. He scored his only two wins in 1966 and finished fifth in points in 1972. As a small-budget independent driver, Langley spent his career driving with used engines and parts. He retired as a driver in 1981, rented his car to drivers for another five seasons, served as Cale Yarborough's crew chief for one year, then joined NASCAR as an inspector and the pace car driver in 1988. His life and racing career ended when he suffered a fatal heart attack while NASCAR was making its first-ever racing appearance in Japan.

FRED LORENZEN

FRED LORENZEN
1934–

At the age of 13, Fred Lorenzen launched his racing career by building a car out of spare parts and an old washing machine engine. Several years later, Lorenzen advanced quickly from demolition derbies to Modifieds to USAC stock cars to NASCAR's premier Winston Cup series. That's where Lorenzen hooked up with the famed Holman-Moody Ford team. Although he never ran a full season, "Fast Freddie" became one of the toughest drivers to beat. Lorenzen made only 158 career starts, but he won 26 races and had 75 top-five finishes. In 1963, Lorenzen was the first driver to earn $100,000 in a season. Over the 1963–64 seasons, he won 14 of the 45 races he started, and finished 13th in Winston Cup points in 1964 despite skipping 45 of the season's 61 races. Lorenzen was just 32 when he first retired from racing in 1967. He returned three years later and raced part-time for three more seasons.

TINY LUND
1936–1975

DeWayne Lund is far better known for an act of heroism than for his exploits on the track. In 1963 at Daytona International Speedway, Lund was watching a sports car practice when Marvin Panch's Maseratti flipped and burst into flames. Lund pulled Panch from the burning wreckage, saving his life. When Panch was unable to race in the Daytona 500, the Wood brothers asked Lund to climb into their Ford. He did, and won the race, one of his two NASCAR Winston Cup victories. The six-foot-five-inch, 270-pound Lund won four championships in NASCAR's Grand American division. Late in his career, Lund raced in Japan as an ambassador for NASCAR.

TINY LUND

M

DAVE MARCIS
1941–

One of the more respected figures in NASCAR Winston Cup racing, Dave Marcis ranks second only to Richard Petty in career starts. After winning the short-track championship in

DAVE MARCIS

his native Wisconsin in 1965, Marcis made his Winston Cup debut in 1968 as an owner-driver. He scored the first of his five career wins in 1975 at Martinsville, Virginia, while driving for Norm Krauskopf. He won three races in 1976 and finished sixth in points. His final win came in 1982 at Richmond, Virginia. Midway through that season, Marcis, who again was also car owner, led the season points race. He finished sixth. He is well known for driving in wingtip shoes.

JOHN MARCUM
1918–1985

It was a chance meeting with Bill France before the inaugural 1936 race on the Beach-Road course at Daytona Beach, Florida, that launched a lifelong friendship and John Marcum's entry into promoting races. At the time, Marcum was one of the country's top young sprint car drivers. But a 1939 accident that hospitalized him for three months with a head injury and World War II changed his direction from driver to promoter. Two years after France formed NASCAR, he appointed Marcum the organization's chief steward for Ohio. In 1953, Marcum decided there needed to be a series headquartered in the Midwest and formed the Midwest Association for Race Cars (MARC). In 1964, MARC was reorganized and renamed the Automobile Racing Club of America (ARCA). The series became a training ground for great drivers,

MARK MARTIN

many of whom got their first taste of superspeedway racing in ARCA's annual visits to Daytona and Talladega superspeedways.

MARK MARTIN
1959–

Considered one of the most versatile drivers in stock car racing, Mark Martin is a four-time American Speed Association champion, a four-time International Race of Champions titlist, and the all-time leader in NASCAR Busch Grand National Series victories, in addition to being one of the top drivers on the NASCAR Winston Cup tour. The native of Batesville, Arkansas, won his first ASA title in 1978 at the age of 19. After winning his third straight ASA title in 1980, Martin ran in the Winston Cup Series as an owner-driver in 1982 and finished 14th in points. After winning his fourth

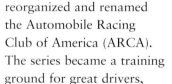

JOHN MARCUM

ASA title in 1986, Martin returned to Winston Cup racing in 1988 with Jack Roush as the owner. Martin has more than 100 wins in major stock car races in ASA, IROC, and NASCAR Winston Cup and Busch Grand National events.

BANJO MATTHEWS
1932–1997

Edwin K. Matthews got his unusual nickname because the thick and very strong glasses he needed looked like twin banjos, which made him an unlikely racer. But Banjo Matthews climbed into his first jalopy at the age of 15 in Pompano Beach, Florida. He soon became one of NASCAR's top modified drivers and won 50 races in 1954. Three times he won the season's premier event at Daytona Beach, Florida, twice on the Beach-Road course (1955 and 1958) and in the 1959 inaugural at Daytona International Speedway. Banjo then advanced to what is now

BANJO MATTHEWS

NASCAR's premier Winston Cup Series. Although he never won a Winston Cup race and had only one top-three finish and three poles in 51 starts before retiring as a driver at the age of 31, Matthews' mark on the series can be seen to this day. He was an expert at building cars and created chassis as a car owner that Fireball Roberts, Junior Johnson, A. J. Foyt, and Donnie Allison occasionally drove in major races. Matthews also designed and built chassis for the Holman-Moody team before he opened his own shop and began making tube-frame chassis for all teams.

HERSHEL McGRIFF
1927–

An Oregon lumberman who loved southern stock car racing, Hershel McGriff started racing in 1945 in his hometown of Portland, then ventured south in 1950 to finish ninth in the first Southern 500 at Darlington, South Carolina. After striking up a friendship with Bill France Sr., McGriff accepted the challenge of the NASCAR founder and ran and won the 1950 Pan-American Road Race. In 1954, McGriff raced the full Winston Cup season for the only time, winning four races and finishing sixth in points. McGriff's career

HERSHEL McGRIFF

spanned six decades, during which he helped create NASCAR's Winston West series. He won the 1986 NASCAR Winston West title at the age of 58.

LEO MEHL
1936–

The man who started out as a tire eingineer in 1962 and eventually became worldwide director of racing for Goodyear Tire and Rubber Company, Leo Mehl made motorsport a priority item for one of the country's biggest automotive-related entities. Goodyear dominated many forms of racing, particularly NASCAR, during his tenure, and he guided numerous tire innovations. After his

LEO MEHL

retirement from Goodyear, Mehl took on the executive director position with the new Indy Racing League.

BUD MOORE
1926–

Like many great stock car minds, Bud Moore entered the sport as a driver. But after several bad accidents, he changed his mind and went behind the scenes, becoming one of the great crew chiefs and car preparers in stock car history. Moore started racing in 1947 when he prepared a 1937 Ford Flathead V8 for himself and driver Joe Eubanks. At one point in 1947, the Moore-Eubanks team won 13 straight races. The pair switched to what would become NASCAR's Winston Cup circuit in 1951. After Eubanks retired in 1956, Moore went to work for Buck Baker as crew chief and helped him win ten races and the 1957 championship. Speedy Thompson won the Southern 500 that same year in the second Moore-prepared Chevrolet. Jack Smith won 12 races in 1958 in a Moore-prepared car and Joe Weatherly won back-to-back titles in 1962–63 in cars owned and prepared by Moore. Although Darel Dieringer won the Southern 500 for Moore in 1965, he placed second in five other major races. The following year, Lincoln-Mercury named Bud Moore Engineering its racing outlet. That meant Moore had to build cars for the Trans-Am road racing series, the Winston Cup, and NASCAR's short-track Grand American circuit. By 1969, Moore had cars competing in all three. Moore won the 1968 Grand-Am title with Tiny Lund and the 1970 Trans-Am title with Parnelli Jones (after finishing second in 1969). Since 1971, Moore has concentrated on the Winston Cup Series, where he has won more than 60 races and ranks third on the all-time list in races started.

BUD MOORE

N

GARY NELSON
1953–

Nelson became NASCAR Winston Cup Series director in 1992 and is the sanctioning body's top cop in the garage. He brought an outstanding resume to the job, having won a Winston Cup championship as Bobby Allison's crew chief in 1983 and the Daytona 500 with Allison and Geoff Bodine. The mechanical innovativeness that was Nelson's trademark as one of the sport's top crew chiefs serves him well in his

GARY NELSON

current position. As Winston Cup director, he has refined policies and procedures and developed a new approach to the approval process for new car models.

O

ED OTTO
1904–1996

A key promoter of automobile and motorcycle racing in the Northeast in the 1940s, Otto became a 20 percent stockholder

ED OTTO

in NASCAR in 1950 as Bill France Sr. sought to increase the organization's influence and visibility outside the Southeast. Bill Tuthill, one of three original NASCAR stockholders, had given part of his stock to Otto to entice him into the fold. A few years later, France and Otto bought Tuthill's share, then France bought out Otto in 1963.

COTTON OWENS
1924–

Called "Cotton" for his white hair, Everett Owens had three careers in stock car racing. Returning to South Carolina after serving in the Navy in World War II, Owens went to work for car owner Gober Sosebee as a mechanic on a modified. In 1947, Sosebee offered Owens a chance to drive one of the cars he had prepared. Owens won more than 200 modified races, including a run of 24 straight in 1951. Although he fancied modifieds more than stock cars as a driver, Owens finished seventh in the inaugural Southern 500 in 1950 at Darlington, South Carolina. He

COTTON OWENS

started competing regularly in what became the NASCAR Winston Cup Series in 1957 and won nine races before he stopped driving in 1962. Owens then returned to his first love of working on cars. In 1963, he owned five cars and in 1966 was the owner and crew chief of the Dodge that David Pearson drove to his first championship. Later he owned cars driven by A. J. Foyt and singer Marty Robbins.

P

MARVIN PANCH
1926–

Marvin Panch never started out to be a racer. His loves were baseball and football and his first foray into professional sports was as a boxer. But after taking a job in an Oakland, California, garage after high school, Panch discovered he was a skilled mechanic and soon began building jalopies for the

California circuit. When his driver didn't appear one Saturday night in 1947, Panch jumped behind the wheel because he wanted to keep the money rather than split it with a backup driver. After winning back-to-back California NASCAR Late Model championships in 1950–51, Panch interrupted his driving career for two years due to a stint in the army. When he returned, he moved to Charlotte, North Carolina, to try the Winston Cup tour. In 1957, Marvin Panch became

MARVIN PANCH

the first driver from the West Coast to make a major impact on what had been traditionally a southern sport dominated by southern drivers when he won six races and finished second in the final NASCAR Winston Cup championship standings in 1957. Panch used his winnings to buy a farm and a business near Daytona Beach, Florida.

RAYMOND PARKS
1914–

Atlanta, Georgia, businessman Raymond Parks was one of the first successful full-time car owners in stock car racing. His run began in 1939 through an association with mechanic Red Vogt and picked up steam after the end of World War II.

RAYMOND PARKS

His drivers included Roy Hall, Lloyd Seay, Red Byron, and brothers Bob and Fonty Flock. When Parks' team arrived at a track, he'd always bring an extra car that sometimes was driven by Bill France Sr., who later became the founder of NASCAR. Parks ran a very professional organization. He would appear at tracks wearing a suit and tie and driving a Cadillac. He struck the same deal with all his drivers. Parks bought the cars, paid all the expenses and the crew, and split the purse evenly with the drivers. Parks also kept all the trophies, which quickly lined the walls of Parks Novelty Machine Company, which rented pinball machines. Byron won the first race sanctioned by NASCAR in a Parks car. Parks, Byron, and Vogt also teamed to win the first season championship in 1948, and the forerunner of the modern Winston Cup Series in 1949. Parks quit racing in 1950.

WALLY PARKS
1909–

It was while attending high school in Southern California that Wally Parks first became interested in cars and speed. He would rebuild stripped-down Model T Fords into hot rods for speed trials on nearby streets and the dry lakes of the neighboring Mojave Desert. In 1937, Parks helped form the Southern California Timing Association, the oldest active organization of hot rod car clubs in the world. A decade later, Parks helped establish *Hot Rod* magazine and in 1949 he led the campaign that opened Utah's Bonneville Salt Flats for hot rod speed trials and, eventually, land speed record attempts. That led to the formation of the National Hot Rod Association in 1951. Parks used his influence as editorial director of five performance

WALLY PARKS

automotive magazines to help build the NHRA into the world's largest motorsport-governing body in terms of members and competitors. Today, the NHRA sanctions 20 national drag racing meets a year. Parks was drag racing's first inductee into the Motorsports Hall of Fame at Talladega, Alabama. In 1992, at the age of 83, Parks re-created the 1957 Plymouth Hot Rod Special in which he had set the world speed record for closed-bodied cars on the beach at Daytona Beach, Florida, and ran it at Bonneville, Utah.

BENNY PARSONS
1941–

The son of a Detroit, Michigan, taxi company owner, Benny Parsons went from driving a cab to racing cars to spinning yarns and becoming a television commentator. As a driver, Parsons claimed 20 poles and won 20 races in a 526-race career. He won the NASCAR Winston Cup title in 1973. His biggest wins were the 1975 Daytona 500 and the 1980 Coca-Cola 600 at Charlotte, North Carolina. He was the first Winston Cup driver to record a 200-mph qualifying lap, accomplishing the feat in 1982 at Talladega, Alabama. But Parsons' greatest contribution to stock car racing has been in his role as a television commentator, where he uses his story-telling ability to make complicated racing concepts easily understood by all fans.

BENNY PARSONS

JIM PASCHAL
1926–

While working for his father as a furniture refinisher, Jim Paschal's main goal in life was to save enough money to buy a chicken farm near his High Point, North Carolina, home. But then some of his buddies talked Paschal into driving in the modified race in 1947 at Daytona Beach, Florida. Paschal won enough money to pay for the trip and enter more modified races. In 1949, he drove his dad's Ford in NASCAR's first Strictly Stock race and in 1950 he raced in the first Southern 500, although he wasn't a tour regular until 1953. Paschal

JIM PASCHAL

spent most of his first dozen years on the Winston Cup circuit in underpowered Hudsons, Fords, Pontiacs, Plymouths, and Mercurys but managed to finish in the top ten of the final standings nine times. Then he hooked up with Petty Enterprises in 1964, when Lee Petty decided to run a second car as a backup for Richard. Paschal won the

DAVID PEARSON

infamous 1964 World 600 at Charlotte, North Carolina, for the Petty team. He again won the World 600 in 1967, the year that saw on-track temperatures soar to 138 degrees. Paschal retired in 1972 with 25 Winston Cup wins to his credit.

DAVID PEARSON
1934–

Called the "Silver Fox" for his cool and cunning driving style as well as his prematurely graying hair, David Pearson ranks second to Richard Petty on many NASCAR Winston Cup lists. During his career, Pearson won 105 races and claimed 113 poles. He won 18 percent of his 574 starts and finished in the top five an astounding 52 percent of the time. Pearson's style was to qualify high, hang close to the lead, and charge at the end. Pearson's famed battles with Petty drew national attention to the sport, climaxing with the 1976 Daytona 500 when the pair crashed nearing the finish on national television.

Pearson won. Only five times during his career did Pearson run a full season. And he won the Winston Cup title in three of those (1966, '68 and '69). The latter two titles came in a Holman-Moody Ford. Later, he won 43 races with the Wood brothers.

ROGER PENSKE
1937–

Although Roger Penske is better known for his efforts in IndyCar racing, where his drivers had won ten Indy 500s, nine national championships, and 99 races going into the

ROGER PENSKE

2000 season, he started his racing career in sports cars. Penske built the first powerhouse team in the Trans-Am Series with Mark Donohue as his driver. Teaming with sponsor Sunoco, Donohue won 29 races and three Trans-Am titles, with two runnerup finishes, from 1967–71. Penske won a fourth Trans-Am title in 1972 with George Follmer. Fielding Chevrolet Camaros and AMC Javelins, he was the most successful owner in Trans-Am racing, and also won five NASCAR Winston Cup races with Donohue and Bobby Allison before turning his focus to IndyCar racing in 1977. After 11 years away from the NASCAR Winston Cup Series, Penske returned in 1990 and has teamed with driver Rusty Wallace ever since. In addition to fielding cars that have won more than 200 races, Penske built the Michigan and California speedways.

LEE PETTY
1914–2000

A mechanic by trade and a devout family man, Lee Petty was patriarch of the "first family" of stock car racing. Petty raced only as a hobby before NASCAR and did not participate in the moonshining trade that launched so many stock car careers. He entered NASCAR's first Strictly Stock race in 1949 at Charlotte, North Carolina, in the family's 1946 Buick, which he had driven from their Level Cross, North Carolina, home, and rolled during the race. Petty always raced his own equipment

LEE PETTY

and made his mark getting underpowered Plymouths to the winner's circle. He was the first three-time champion on NASCAR's premier series (1954, '58, and '59). Petty was also instrumental in making early stock cars safer and helped develop such innovations as roll bars and driver's-side window webs. When he retired as a driver in 1964, he was the Winston Cup win leader with 54. He still ranks seventh in the all-time rankings.

RICHARD PETTY
1937–

Known simply as "The King," Richard Petty is the greatest stock car racer who ever lived, and he has the numbers to show it: 200 race wins, seven NASCAR Winston Cup titles, 126 poles. His career spanned 35 years, running from NASCAR's formative days to the modern era. He started a record 1,184 races. He held

the lead in 599 of those starts and led 52,194 laps of the incredible 307,836 he completed. Richard began driving for his father's team in 1958 and became the primary driver of the Petty Enterprises empire in 1961. He won his first NASCAR title in 1964 at a time when interest in stock car racing was beginning to branch out from its southern roots. Petty helped the growth. His oversized hat, dark sunglasses, and huge grin, along with the family's "Petty Blue" No. 43 cars,

RICHARD PETTY

became as identifiable as the sport itself. One particular season stands out in the Petty legend: In 1967, he won a record 27 of the season's 48 races, including 10 in a row.

R

TIM RICHMOND
1955–1989

Tim Richmond was the first great driver to jump from open-wheel IndyCar racing to

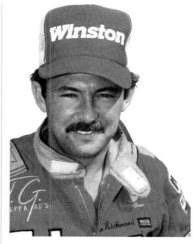

TIM RICHMOND

NASCAR Winston Cup racing. He made the switch in 1981, the year after he won Rookie of the Year honors at the

Indianapolis 500. For a while, Richmond competed in both stock cars and IndyCars, impressing fans with his versatility. He was best known for his ability on NASCAR's road courses. Five of his 13 career NASCAR Winston Cup victories and three of his 14 poles came on those courses, including a sweep of both races at Riverside, California, in 1982. In 1986, Richmond teamed with car owner Rick Hendrick and finished third in

the final NASCAR Winston Cup standings with seven wins and 11 top-three finishes. He died in 1989 after a lengthy illness.

LES RICHTER
1930–

Born and raised in Fresno, California, Les Richter is affectionately known as "Coach" throughout racing circles. His background was far from racing. An honors student in business and economics at the University of California where he also starred in football, Richter was a standout linebacker with the Los Angeles Rams in 1960 when club owner Edwin Pauley encouraged him to become the executive director of nearby Riverside International Raceway. Richter's business acumen turned the struggling facility into a profit maker. When the area's expanding population forced the raceway to close in 1983, Richter became chairman of the International Race of Champions. He then became senior vice president for operations of NASCAR.

LES RICHTER

FIREBALL ROBERTS
1929–1964

Glenn Roberts was the first superstar of stock car racing. Fast and daring on the track, the college-educated Roberts was articulate and quick-witted off it. He was the first stock car driver to be routinely quoted. And there was a lot to talk about. Ironically, his nickname had nothing to do with racing. He picked up the "Fireball" tag while pitching for the University of Florida, where he studied mechanical engineering. His educational background helped Roberts understand cars and the art of tweaking suspensions. His 32 NASCAR Winston Cup wins included four each at Daytona and Darlington, making Roberts the early king of the superspeedways. However, he is best known for a race he didn't win. In 1959, Roberts started the inaugural Daytona 500 from the 46th spot. He

took the lead 23 laps into the race only to later withdraw with a failed fuel pump. Roberts died in 1964 of injuries suffered in the World 600 at Charlotte, North Carolina.

T. WAYNE ROBERTSON
1949–1998

He never raced a car, never owned a race car and never turned a wrench on one. But Wayne Robertson was one of the more influential men in the rapid growth of American stock

T. WAYNE ROBERTSON

car and drag racing. A 27-year employee of R. J. Reynolds Tobacco Company, Robertson led RJR's Sports Marketing Enterprises for 14 years during an era when NASCAR's Winston Cup Series and the National Hot Rod Association's Winston Drag Racing became well-known names in the sports industry. A native of Winston-Salem, North Carolina, Robertson joined R. J. Reynolds in

FIREBALL ROBERTS

JACK ROUSH

1971 as a show car driver and administrative trainee. He worked his way up through the organization and became director of special events in 1984, overseeing R. J. Reynolds' campaigns in everything from racing to golf to tennis. But the biggest programs were Winston's associations with NASCAR and drag racing. Robertson oversaw the Winston Cup expansion and developed the Winston all-star race format. In 1990, he was honored by *The Sporting News* as one of the 50 most powerful people in sports.

JACK ROUSH
1942–

Armed with a master's degree in mathematics, Jack Roush joined Ford's engineering department in 1964. While working in the assembly and trim division, Roush joined the Fastbacks – a dozen Ford technical people who drag raced Mustangs, Fairlanes, and Galaxies in the National Hot Rod Association's Stock and Pro Stock divisions. In 1969,

Roush's interest in race cars got a boost when he joined Chrysler's Advanced Development Division. In 1971, he formed a racing-oriented engineering company with Wayne Gapp and won International Hot Rod Association Pro Stock titles in 1973 and 1974. Although the partnership ended in 1975 and Roush didn't return to racing until 1983, the foundation was laid for creation of one of the most powerful teams in American racing history. Based in Livonia, Michigan, Jack Roush Performance Engineering won more than 100 races (including nine straight 24 Hours of Daytona GTO titles), and 21 championships in Sports Car Club of America and International Motor Sports Association sports car series. In 1988, Roush's association with driver Mark Martin led to the formation of a NASCAR Winston Cup team. Roush added a second car in 1992, a third in 1996, a fourth in 1997, and a fifth in 1999.

RICKY RUDD
1956–

The son of a salvage yard operator, Ricky Rudd spent his youth going through old cars and parts. During the early days of his Winston Cup career, he drove a car owned by his father, Al. Although he later raced for such respected owners as Richard Childress, Bud Moore, and Rick Hendrick (with whom he finished second in the final points standings in 1991), it was Rudd's dream to be an owner-driver. Six seasons produced as many wins and three top-ten points finishes. The end of the 1999 season marked several watershed events for Ricky Rudd. He went without a victory in 1999, ending a streak that saw him get at least one Winston Cup Series victory in a NASCAR modern-era-record 16 straight seasons. At the end of the 1999 season, Rudd also ended his six-year run as an owner-driver and joined the Robert Yates team as teammate to Winston Cup champion Dale Jarrett.

RALPH SEAGRAVES

RALPH SEAGRAVES
1927–1996

He never drove a car or worked in a garage, but Ralph Seagraves played a vital role in the growth of stock car racing. Shortly after becoming the head of Reynolds Tobacco's Special Events Operations in 1972, Seagraves forged sponsorship relationships with NASCAR and the National Hot Rod Association. The most notable result in stock car racing was the creation of NASCAR's Winston Cup Series. Not only did Seagraves put together a sponsorship package, he also worked with NASCAR to streamline the series, eliminating some smaller and mid-week events and adding emphasis to each week's race. This was the beginning of NASCAR's modern era. Seagraves also worked with tracks around the country to improve facilities and racing at the grassroots level, and he helped racing teams create links to other corporate sponsors.

LLOYD SEAY
1920–1941

Seay was one of the best stock car drivers to never participate in a Winston Cup event. One

LLOYD SEAY

of a crowd of great racers to come out of the hill country of northern Georgia, Seay drove fast cars owned by Atlanta businessman Raymond Parks

to dozens of dirt-track victories. He was shot and killed September 2, 1941, after an apparent argument over a payment related to an illegal whiskey delivery run. He was 21. Bill France Jr. once called him "probably the Dale Earnhardt of 1941."

BRUTON SMITH

BRUTON SMITH
1926–

Once a dirt-track promoter in the Carolinas, Smith has become of the most important people in international motorsport. Chairman of Speedway Motorsports Inc., Smith is the prime mover and shaker in tracks at Charlotte, North Carolina; Fort Worth, Texas; Bristol, Tennessee; Atlanta, Georgia; Las Vegas, Nevada; and Sonoma, California, and has been one of racing's greatest innovators. Builder of Lowe's Motor Speedway and Texas Motor Speedway, two of auto racing's most modern and successful tracks, Smith has made bold moves where others feared to tread.

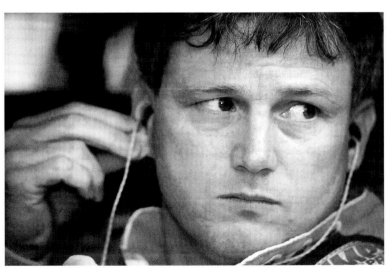

RICKY RUDD

GOBER SOSEBEE

GOBER SOSEBEE
1915–1997

Gober Sosebee grew up in the fertile racing community that developed in and around Atlanta in the 1930s and '40s and became one of the leading dirt-track drivers of the 1950s. He won Winston Cup races in 1952 and '54 and scored 33 top tens in a nine-year career at NASCAR's top level. He was killed in a farm tractor accident in 1996 at the age of 81.

KEN SQUIER
1938–

Car racing fans first heard the voice of Ken Squier in 1952. He was 14 and calling the action at a small track in his native Vermont. By the age of 17, Squier was promoting races at state fairs and, for six years, also spent time behind the wheel as a driver. He built and operated two small tracks in New England while doing play-by-play radio announcing for baseball and boxing. Squier's break in broadcasting came in 1965 when he was named the public address announcer for Daytona

International Speedway. Four years later, Squier became a founder and a principal voice of radio's Motor Racing Network. Television was also getting into stock car racing at the time and Squier joined CBS Sports in 1972. It was with CBS that Squier became the play-by-play announcer of the Daytona 500, Michigan 500, and Talladega 500, opening the world of NASCAR Winston Cup racing to a legion of new fans.

KEN SQUIER

MARSHALL TEAGUE
1922–1959

Having grown up on the ocean side of Daytona Beach, Florida, Marshall Teague knew the tricky sands and tides of the famed 4.7-mile Beach-Road course better than anyone. So it was no surprise that Teague became known as the King of the Beach. He won the 1949 Modified race on the beach and scored two of his seven Winston Cup victories

MARSHALL TEAGUE

there. But Marshall Teague was far more than a beach racer. Skilled at both tuning engines and preparing a chassis, Teague prepared the Hudson Hornets that he and teammate Herb Thomas used to dominate stock car racing in the early '50s. He poured so much into the cars that they became known among racers as

Teaguemobiles. While Thomas competed on the NASCAR tour, Teague switched to the rival AAA (later USAC) series and won the championship in 1952 and '54 and was second in 1953. Teague also competed in Indy Cars (he was seventh in the 1957 Indy 500) and died February 11, 1959 while testing an Indy Car at Daytona International Speedway.

HERB THOMAS
1923–

Herb Thomas loved to drive. He drove trucks before he drove stock cars. And he returned to truck driving as the owner of his own company after he retired as a racer. In between stints on the open road, Thomas was one of NASCAR's first legends. Thomas was NASCAR's first two-time Winston Cup champion, winning the title in 1951 in a Hudson Hornet and and repeating two years later in the boxy but sturdy sedan. Early in his career, Thomas

HERB THOMAS

CURTIS TURNER

won in cars he owned and prepared and teamed with Marshall Teague. Later he drove Chryslers for Carl Kiekhaefer. The first three-time winner of the Southern 500 at Darlington, South Carolina (1951, '54, and '55), Thomas won 48 races and 39 poles in 230 starts. A series of bad accidents in the late 1950s cut short his racing career and returned Thomas to trucks and the open highway.

CURTIS TURNER
1924–1970

Perhaps the most flamboyant character of NASCAR's formative years, and close friend of Bill France Sr. who teamed with the NASCAR founder in the 1950 Pan-American Road Race, Curtis Turner later drew a four-year probation from France for trying to organize a drivers' union. Turner was also an astute businessman away from racing who harvested lumber and owned real estate. He helped build Charlotte Motor Speedway. A native of Roanoke,

Virginia, Turner won the fourth race of NASCAR's original season and is credited with 17 NASCAR Winston Cup victories. But estimates put Turner's career wins in stock cars at more than 300 and he raced the USAC circuit from 1962 until his NASCAR reinstatement in 1965. At the age of 41, in just his second race back, Turner out-battled Cale Yarborough to win the first race at Rockingham, North Carolina.

RED VOGT
1909–1984

It was Red Vogt and not Bill France Sr. who thought up the name NASCAR during the organization's 1947 organizational meeting. That was not surprising since Vogt assisted France on many issues during NASCAR's formative years. Vogt helped establish the prerace inspections that became a cornerstone for

NASCAR's acceptance with drivers. A native of Atlanta, Vogt moved to Daytona Beach to be closer to NASCAR's base. He served as crew chief for two of NASCAR's earliest teams owned by Raymond Parks and Carl Kiekhaefer. Bill France himself once drove a Vogt-prepared car. So did the three Flock brothers and pioneer NASCAR champion Red Byron. During NASCAR's early days, Vogt was often the voice of the unheard – the mechanics and crewmen who prepared the cars.

RED VOGT

RUSTY WALLACE

W

RUSTY WALLACE
1956–

The son of a three-time Missouri track champion, Rusty Wallace ran both USAC (Rookie of the Year) and ASA (1983 champion) series before arriving on NASCAR's Winston Cup circuit in 1980. After running only nine races in his first four seasons, Wallace's first full campaign produced Rookie of the Year honors in 1984. Wallace won NASCAR's 1989 Winston Cup title and placed second in 1988 and 1993 when he won a career-best ten races. Wallace is considered one of the modern tour's top short-track racers and is the all-time co-leader in road course wins with six. Although he won his title while driving for former drag race champion Raymond Beadle, more than half of Rusty's career wins came for car owner Roger Penske. Rusty's brothers Mike and Kenny also drove in the Winston Cup Series.

DARRELL WALTRIP
1947–

When he retired after the 2000 season, Darrell Waltrip ranked third in career NASCAR Winston Cup Series wins with 84. But the three-time Winston Cup champion played a much bigger role in NASCAR's growth than just winning races. The articulate and outspoken Waltrip was a natural in front of the television cameras at a time when television became a partner in stock car racing's growth. As a driver, Waltrip flourished during his partnership with car owner Junior Johnson, who fielded all three of Waltrip's championship cars. Waltrip won back-to-back titles in 1981–82, his 12 wins in both seasons being the most since Richard Petty won 13 races in 1975. Waltrip won 8 races from the pole in 1981 and had 21 top-three finishes in 31 starts. He won his third title in 1985. Waltrip scored 43 wins and 34 poles in his six seasons with Johnson.

JOE WEATHERLY
1922–1964

A three-time flat-track grand national champion of the American Motorcyclist Association before he turned to cars, the versatile Joe Weatherly was one of NASCAR's earliest superstars. He won NASCAR's Modified Division in 1953, capping a two-season blitz that saw him win 101 races. From 1956 to 1959, Weatherly raced in NASCAR's Convertible Division. He joined what is now NASCAR's Winston Cup Series in 1960 and claimed 19 poles and 25 races in 230 starts. Weatherly won back-to-back Winston Cup titles in 1962 (in Bud Moore's Pontiac) and 1963 (in a Mercury). Weatherly died in a 1964 accident at Riverside International Raceway in California.

JOE WEATHERLY

BOB WELBORN
1928–1997

It was during the late 1950s, when convertibles were the rage with car buyers, that Bob Welborn was as well known in stock car racing circles as the champions of NASCAR's premier series. Welborn got his start in modifieds and finished fourth in the 1955 Winston Cup Series. He won nine races and had seven poles in 183 Winston Cup starts. But his mark was in convertibles. Back then, NASCAR's Convertible Series was almost parallel to the featured Winston Cup Series. Welborn won 26 races and three straight Convertible titles from 1956 to 1958 before NASCAR discontinued the series. At one time, Welborn held 20 qualifying and race records.

BOB WELBORN

HUMPY WHEELER
1939–

The P. T. Barnum of stock car racing, Humpy Wheeler has redefined the word "promotion" in motorsport. Signing on with track owner Bruton Smith to

DARRELL WALTRIP

HUMPY WHEELER

run Charlotte Motor Speedway in 1975, Wheeler used his considerable marketing and promotional skills to make the track one of the world's motorsport capitals. Using innovative ideas, including the then-revolutionary notion of lighting the speedway for night racing in 1992, Wheeler has become perhaps the leading expert on expanding motorsport's reach into new arenas and new ideas.

DON WHITE
1926–

Known as the Keokuk Komet for his Iowa roots, Don White was to stock car racing in the Midwest what Richard Petty was to the South. And, like Petty, the Midwestern "king" drove Dodge products through most of his career. White's favorite car was the Dodge Charger. White is the all-time win leader on the United States Stock Car circuit with 53. That is 12 more wins than runnerup A. J. Foyt, who battled White many times on USAC's dirt ovals at state fairs. White won two USAC stock car championships, in 1963 and 1967.

REX WHITE

REX WHITE
1929–

While many of NASCAR's pioneers learned their trade running moonshine on back-country roads, Rex White developed his smooth style delivering eggs around Taylorsville, North Carolina. And getting a load of eggs to market over the treacherous roads was no simple matter, particularly for the 5'4" White, who had trouble reaching the pedals of the cars of the era. But Rex White became one of NASCAR's top short-track racers at a time when titles were determined on short tracks. He won 28 races in his career and was second in NASCAR's Short-Track Series in 1958 and 1959. He was the 1960 champion of what became NASCAR's Winston Cup Series. He finished second in the 1961 Winston Cup standings.

White and chief mechanic-car owner Louis Clements turned their success with their Chevrolet race cars into a business association with one of the South's top speed shops in Spartanburg, South Carolina. White's only superspeedway win came in the 1962 Dixie 400 at Atlanta. White's key to success was his consistency. He finished in the top five in 10 of the 233 races he started.

WADDELL WILSON
1936–

Waddell Wilson started work on the Holman-Moody racing engine assembly line in 1963 and became one of motorsport's most respected engine builders. Wilson built winning engines for Fred Lorenzen, David Pearson, Bobby Allison, Benny

WADDELL WILSON

Parsons, A. J. Foyt, Curtis Turner, and Junior Johnson, among others. Wilson's engine room knowledge put him into a position to be a crew chief, consultant, and general manager for several top teams. He began the 2000 season as general manager of A. J. Foyt's new Winston Cup team.

DON WHITE

LEONARD WOOD AND GLEN WOOD
1928– AND 1924–

Although they are respected as the Wood brothers, it was Glen who started it all as an owner-driver of a modified back in 1950. Glen was the North Carolina Sportsman champion in 1954, placed third in NASCAR's convertible series in 1957, was voted NASCAR's most popular driver in 1959, and won three Winston Cup races in 1960. By 1964, Wood and his brothers had decided to go in another direction as owners and crewmen of a team. For a while, the team included brothers Glen, Ray, Leonard, Delano, and Clay, as well as cousin Ralph Edwards and a friend named Ken Martin. The six-man crew revolutionized the way race cars were serviced during races. Led by Glen and Leonard, the team organized every aspect of the pit stop and choreographed

assignments against a stop watch. They became overnight sensations, and the crew had as many fans as drivers. Wood Brothers' pit stops were a third as long as their rivals – and not only in Winston Cup stock car racing. In 1965, Jimmy Clark won the Indy 500 thanks in part to the Wood Brothers' pit crew, who spent a total of 44.5 seconds on two stops. Such drivers as Marvin Panch, Dan Gurney, A. J. Foyt, Cale Yarborough, David Pearson, and Neil Bonnett drove the famed Wood Brothers Mercurys. Pearson won 42 races for the Wood brothers.

CALE YARBOROUGH
1939–

In a word, Cale Yarborough is tough. Before he reached maturity, he was struck by both a rattlesnake and

CALE YARBOROUGH

lightning. He skipped college and went directly from being a high school football star to a standout for a semipro team. He took up skydiving when the odds weren't with the parachutist and once wrestled an alligator. And, as one of the greatest chargers in stock car racing history, he was at his best in NASCAR's most famed races. Yarborough is a four-time winner of the Daytona 500 and a five-time winner of the Southern 500 at Darlington, which is just down the road from his Timmonsville, South Carolina, home. Driving for Junior Johnson, Yarborough is the only driver to win three straight NASCAR Winston Cup titles (1976–78). Yarborough won 15 percent of his 559 starts, his 83 career wins ranking him fifth on the all-time victory list. Yarborough ranks third with 70 poles and is tied for third with 47

superspeedway wins. But he ranks second in laps led (31,776). How he did it was almost as important as what Yarborough did. After retiring as a driver in 1988, he continued on as a car owner for another 11 seasons.

LEEROY YARBROUGH
1938–1984

LeeRoy Yarbrough didn't just want to win, he wanted to win fast. A native of Jacksonville, Florida, Yarbrough lied about his age to launch his racing career at the age of 14. After winning 52 races in one year at a local track, Yarbrough won 32 NASCAR Sportsman races in 1962. In 1969, he had one of the greatest seasons in NASCAR Winston Cup Series history. Each of his seven victories in a Junior Johnson-owned Ford came on a superspeedway, including a sweep of the Daytona 500; the

GLEN WOOD AND LEONARD WOOD

LEEROY YARBROUGH

Southern 500 at Darlington, South Carolina; and the Coca-Cola 600 at Charlotte, North Carolina. Until Yarbrough, the record for superspeedway victories in a season was four. Yarbrough won only 14 races on NASCAR's Winston Cup Series, but he led 66 of the 198 races he started.

ROBERT YATES
1943–

His title is now car owner, but Robert Yates still views himself as a mechanic. Building engines, he believes, is his best skill. And few would argue. Yates is considered one of the top engine builders in stock car racing history. It was while testing his skills as a drag racer in the early 1960s that Robert Yates started tinkering with engines. In 1968, he joined the Holman-Moody team where he worked alongside such engine builders as Waddell

Wilson and Jack Roush. Yates built engines for Junior Johnson's team and such drivers as Darrell Waltrip and Bobby Allison. After working on the development of synthetic fuels for several years during the 1980s, Yates returned to the NASCAR Winston Cup Series in 1987 as the manager of the Ranier-Lundy team. A year later, Yates bought the team and joined forces with a young driver named Davey Allison. The Yates-Allison combination won 15 races in just over four championships and was challenging for the 1993 NASCAR Winston Cup Series title when Allison tragically died in a helicopter accident. Yates' dreams of winning a NASCAR Winston Cup championship were finally answered in 1999 when Dale Jarrett won the title.

SMOKEY YUNICK

SMOKEY YUNICK
1923–

Yunick always considered himself a mechanic by necessity. He was 13 and plowing fields behind a pair of horses near Fayetteville, North Carolina, when the horses got sick and died. Yunick found an old tractor in a nearby junkyard, rebuilt the engine, and drove it home. A year later, he was the leading mechanic in the local garage. A B-17 pilot and veteran of 52 missions in World War II, Yunick moved to Daytona Beach, Florida, in 1947 and opened a garage called "The Best Damn Garage In Town." There perhaps the

ROBERT YATES

greatest, and surely the most controversial, mechanic in stock car racing history went to work. Yunick's battles with NASCAR president Bill France Sr. became legend. Yunick was the type to always try and push the rules. And France was the type to push Yunick, who was as stubborn and opinionated as he was innovative. Yunick built the engines that powered Herb Thomas' Hudsons to season championships in 1952 and '53. Yunick's Pontiacs later won four of the first eight races run on the high banks of the new Daytona International Speedway with Fireball Roberts and Marvin Panch as his drivers. To Yunick, the tires and springs were as important to race cars as the engines were. He took many ideas from sports car racing, and turned wrenches at the Daytona 500 as well as the Indianapolis 500.

Glossary

AERODYNAMICS

The art of designing the body to create smoother air flow around the car, thereby decreasing drag.

A-FRAME

A wheel suspension component named for its shape and designed to hold the wheel securely in its proper location.

APRON

The low, flat-surfaced, inside edge of a race track used only in case of emergency.

ARCA

Automobile Racing Club of America.

ASA

American Speed Association.

BACK-MARKER

The car in last place at the back of the pack.

BANKING

Sloped turns on racing ovals which create a second groove and thus allow cars to run at higher speeds with less braking.

BINDERS

Slang for brakes.

BITE

Traction on a racetrack.

BLOWN ENGINE

Term used to cover a variety of engine failures.

BRAKES

Originally drum-shaped, now disc-shaped with friction-faced pads, devices used to slow or stop car.

BUSCH GRAND NATIONAL

Secondary NASCAR series behind the Winston Cup. Cars are slightly lighter and engines are less powerful.

CAMSHAFT

A shaft with cams (eccentric lobes) mounted on it to drive engine valve gear.

CARBURETOR

Although it has been replaced by fuel injection in passenger cars, this device on top of the engine is still used in NASCAR to mix fuel and air for combustion in cylinders.

CAUTION

The period in which cars are slowed to non-racing speeds and must hold position under a yellow flag so accidents or debris can be safely cleared from the track.

CHASSIS

The main structure of the car, usually a tubular frame. Some hybrid prototypes have monocoque frames of molded carbon fiber.

CONTINGENCY AWARDS

Bonus prizes won by top finishers for carrying decals of certain sponsors.

CORNER

A turn on an oval track.

CRAFTSMAN TRUCKS

NASCAR's newest national series uses Winston Cup engines in full-sized pickup trucks.

CREW CHIEF

The man in charge of preparing the car and overseeing pit and team race strategy.

DRAFTING

The practice of riding in the wind shadow close behind the car just ahead. This allows the trailing car to maintain the same speed as the lead car while using less power and fuel. Two cars running extremely close in this manner will create a vacuum that pulls both along at a higher speed because they create less wind turbulence.

DRAG RACE

Two cars racing side-by-side in a test of acceleration and speed over a short straightaway distance, usually a quarter-mile.

ENGINE

The car's motor. The American standard V8 remains the backbone power plant of stock car racing.

EXHAUST SYSTEM

The exhaust manifold and pipes through which the engine's waste gases flow. A well-tuned exhaust system will boost engine efficiency and horsepower.

FACTORY TEAM

Drivers, owners, and mechanics who receive their financial support from a particular manufacturer.

FAIRING

Smoothed surfaces and corners of the car's body contoured to enhance its aerodynamics.

FIA

Federation Internationale de Automobile; the international sanctioning body in Europe for everything from Formula One to Le Mans-style races.

FIRESUIT

Made of fire-resistant Nomex cloth, a suit which includes gloves and special shoes that protect drivers and pit crews against fire.

FLAGMAN

The official in the raised stand near the start-finish line who controls the race by signalling with the flags.

FLAGS

Shown at the start-finish line, to signal the drivers of track conditions and situations (green=race; yellow=caution; red=stop; black=pit for consultation; blue=move over; white=one lap to go; checkered=first shown to the winner, this flag signals the race is over).

FUEL INJECTION

A system by which fuel is forced into the engine's cylinders, either mechanically or electronically, to improve combustion.

GARAGE

An area in the infield or near a track where cars are prepared before a race, and where major repairs are completed during competition.

GREEN

A new racing surface, or a track that has been washed clean of tire rubber after a period of rain.

GREEN FLAG

When the green flag is shown and the green lights are on, the cars are racing.

GROOVE

The part of the racetrack where cars handle best at top speed.

HEMI

An engine equipped with ahemispherically-shaped combustion chamber to increase horsepower.

HORSEPOWER

Unit used to define the power output of an engine.

IHRA

International Hot Rod Association; the drag racing sanctioning body.

INFIELD

The area inside an oval track.

INTER-LINER

The tire within a tire on stock cars to prevent blowouts.

JACK

Tool used to hike the car during pit stops for tire changes. Three-pump jacks used to be the standard. Modern titanium alloy jacks can lift a car in one pump.

LAP

The distance covered on a closed course from the start line back to the start line.

LAPPED

When the lead car in the races passes the last car on the track.

LATE-MODEL

A stock car that is no more than three years old.

LOOSE

A car tending to drift in a corner rather than turn.

MODERN ERA

Began in 1972 for NASCAR Winston Cup Series when season was shortened, eliminating some smaller races and tracks.

MOPAR

Chrysler products.

NASCAR

National Association for Stock Car Auto Racing; the world's premier stock car sanctioning body.

NHRA

National Hot Rod Association; the top promoter of drag races.

PACE CAR

N
The non-racing car that leads the pack during two or three warmup laps before a race and sets the slower speed during caution-period laps.

PITS

The trackside lane inside the main straightaway where cars are refueled and take on new tires during races.

POLE POSITION

The starting location on the inside of the front row on the starting grid, which usually goes to the fastest qualifier.

PUSH

When the front end of a car forms a tendency to drift toward the outside wall.

PUSH ROD

Rods that push against rockers to open overhead valves in standard V8 stock car engine.

QUALIFYING

Speed trials before the race by which the field is set with faster cars up front and slower ones in back.

RESTRICTOR PLATE

A device which reduces the amount of air flowing into the carburetor, thus reducing horsepower and speed.

RIDE

Slang for getting a driver's spot on a race team.

ROLL CAGE

Hollow alloy tubing that protects the driver from impact. Originally little more than a bar behind and above the driver's head, the modern cage offers almost wrap-around protection.

SHOCKS

Gas-buffered devices that work in conjunction with the car's suspension springs to control bouncing.

SLICKS

Smooth-surfaced racing tires.

SLINGSHOT

The type of pass made coming out of a draft on a high-speed track. The trailing car is usually running at less than full throttle, giving it more potential power when it goes to pass.

SOUP-UP

To modify an engine to increase horsepower.

SPOILERS

Wing-like appendages on the trunk lid and under the nose used to provide downforce and improve a car's handling at high speed.

SUPERCHARGER

An engine-driven compressor that provides forced fuel induction to greatly boost horsepower. Mainly used in drag racing.

SUPERSPEEDWAY

Officially, NASCAR ovals of a mile or longer, but usually used to refer to the high-banked ovals.

SUSPENSION

The springs, shock absorbers, and sway bars between the chassis and wheels used to control the car's ride.

SWAY BAR

A rigid suspension component used to limit a car's side-to-side sway when turning.

TIGHT

Describes a car that is difficult to turn.

TORSION BAR

A device to provide stability to the car's suspension by resisting twisting forces.

TRANS-AM

The road racing series contested in sports sedans.

TRANSMISSION

The gears and drive box used to get the engine's power to the drive wheels.

TRI-OVAL

An oval with a triangulated, banked front stretch, giving fans better views of the entire race track as well as the pits.

VALVES

Engine-driven devices which let air and fuel in and exhaust gases out of engine cylinders during the combustion cycle.

WEDGE

Adjustment made through a roof crank during pit stops to raise or lower corners of the car to shift weight and improve handling.

WINSTON CUP

NASCAR's premier series since 1972. Originally termed Strictly Stock, the class was called Grand National in the period from 1950 to 1971.

Index

Index entries in bold refer to main headings, those in italic refer to illustrations

Acknowledgments

I WOULD LIKE to thank the following for their help and advice: Bob Moore, Bob Latford, Tom Higgins, Buzz McKim, Raymond Park, Richard Petty, Cotton Owens, and Junior Johnson.

Photography by:
George Tiedemann, Kenneth Hawking.

Dorling Kindersley would like to thank the following:
The Daytona Racing Archives; Jim Freeman, Marcus Embry and Harlan Ponder at the Talladega Speedway Museum; Donna and Mark Sisler at the Charlotte Motor Speedway Museum; Francis Segars and Sammie Yarborough at the Darlington Motor Speedway Museum; Teresa Long and Marc Gewertz at the National Hot Rod Association; David Kimble; The Ford Motor Company; Kevin Davey at Davey Sports Management, Inc; the United States Auto Club; Jim Picco; R.L. "Pete" Garramone; Jim Ober at Trackside Photos; and Bruce Badgley.

Dorling Kindersley would also like to thank the following for their kind permission to reproduce the photographs:

a=above; c=centre; b=below; l=left; r=right; t=top;

Allsport USA: Jim Lee 5bl, Mike Powell 24br 128-129bc, 128tl, 128tr, 129bl, 129br, 129tl, David Taylor 26t, Darrel Dennis 70tr; Ken Breslauer: 52tl; Ken Breslauer Collection: 102tl, 120tl, 16t, 54cl, 54tl; Daytona Racing Archives: 4cr, 8bc, 9, 9b, 13t, 14b, 16cb, 17cb, 17t, 18b, 18t, 19c, 20br, 20t, 21c, 22t, 23br, 23t, 30-31cb, 31c, 31b, 32-33, 33, 34-35bc, 34br, 34c, 34tl, 34tr, 35al, 35br, 35tr, 36ar, 36cl, 36cr, 36-37b, 36tl, 37t, 38ar, 38tl, 38-39cr, 39tr, 40ar, 40bl, 40tl, 40-41bc, 41al, 41tr, 43, 44, 44tr, 44-45, 44cl, 45c, 45t, 46-47c, 46ar, 47br, 47t, 48ar, 48bl, 48c, 49t, 50-51bl, 50-51c, 51, 50bl, 50tl, 50tr, 51tr, 52c, 54c, 55c, 56b, 56c, 56tl, 57b, 56-57b, 57t, 58c, 58tl, 58tr, 58-59bc, 59, 59br, 59c, 60tl, 60tr, 61br, 62cl, 62tr, 63t, 64, 65, 66c, 66tl, 67tr, 70cl, 71cl, 71tl, 72c, 72tc, 72tl, 72-73bc, 73, 73tr, 74cl, 74tr, 74-75b, 75cl, 75t, 76cl, 76tl, 76tr, 76-77bc, 77tl, 77tr, 78tl, 78tr, 80cl, 80tr, 82, 84c, 86cl, 86tl, 86-87ac, 86-87bc, 87cr, 87tr, 88tl, 88tr, 89c, 89t, 90-91c, 90bl, 90tr, 91br, 91t, 92-93bc, 92bl, 93t, 94c, 94tl, 94tr, 95c, 95t, 96, 97, 98-99, 102tr, 102-103br, 103cr, 104tr, 104bl, 104cl, 104tl, 106b, 107c, 106-107tc, 106cl, 107cr, 107tr, 108-109bc, 108cl, 108tr, 109, 109, 10bl, 10c, 110-111bc, 110tr, 111cr, 114c, 114tl, 115br, 115t, 116cl, 117cr, 117t, 118-119c, 118br, 118tr, 119br, 11tr, 120tr, 122bl, 122tl, 124tr, 124tl, 124, 124-125bc, 125c, 125tr, 126-127bc, 126tl, 12bl, 12tr, 136-137bc, 136tr, 144acl, 144cl, 154, 155, 156bl, 156c, 156br, 157br, 157tc, 157bl, 157c, 158br, 158cl, 158tc, 158tl, 159c, 159br, 161br, 161c, 161t, 162bl, 162bc, 162c, 162tr, 163cl, 163cr, 163t, 164bc, 164c, 164cl, 165br, 165cl, 165cr, 166cl, 166bcr, 166tl, 166tr, 167br, 167bc, 167tc, 167cl, 168bcl, 168bcr, 168c, 168cr, 169bcl, 169br, 169tl, 169cr, 170bc, 170tr, 170cl, 171br, 171c, 171tc, 171tl, 172c, 172br, 172tr, 172cl, 173bcl, 173tc, 173br, 174cl, 174tc, 175br, 175c, 175tc, 175tr, 176c, 176bl, 176tr, 177cr, 177bc, 177bl, 177tc, 178br, 178tc, 178c, 178tl, 179c, 179tr, 179br, 180c, 180tr, 181bcr, 181bl, 181tc, 181tl, 183tr, 183tl, 183bc; Ford Motor Company: 146-147c; R. L. Garramone: 68tl, 68tr, 69tr, 69tl; Kenneth Hawking: 1, 134-135bc, 134c, 134tr, 135, 135tl, 135tr; Don Hunter: 92tr, 99t;

David Kimble: 61a, 62-63c, 100-101, 132-133b, 144-145c; Ron Lewis Photos: 81tr; Jonathan V. Mauk: 42-43; Dozier Mobley: 126cr; Motorsports: Badgley 148c, 148tr, 148-149bc, 149tr; National Hot Rod Association: 14tl, 15c, 68-69bc, 69t, 116bl, 132tl, 133t; James Picco Collection: 132bl; George Tiedemann: 2b, 2c, 2t, , 4bl, 5cr, 6, 24t, 25c, 26b, 27t, 28b, 28t, 29b, 36bl, 39, 38bl, 39bl, 39br, 46bl, 48tl, 48-49b, 49, 49cl, 49cr, 52tr, 52-53bc, 53cr, 53tl, 54tr, 54-55bc, 55tr, 56tl, 59t, 60-61b, 66bl, 66t, 66-67b, 67tl, 67tl, 67tl, 67tl, 70-71b, 70tl, 71, 71tr, 78-79c, 78bl, 79br, 79tc, 79tr, 80-81c, 80tl, 81br, 81tl, 83, 88-89b, 88bl, 92tl, 94-95bc, 99, 98tr, 99cr, 102bl, 103, 103tr, 104-105bc, 108tl, 109, 110bl, 110c, 110tl, 111br, 111tl, 112, 113, 114tr, 114-115bc, 116tl, 116tr, 116-117c, 117br, 118bl, 118cl, 119cr, 119tl, 120bl, 120-121bc, 121br, 121t, 122tr, 122-123bc, 123c, 123t, 126tr, 127t, 130, 131, 132tr, 136cl, 136tl, 137t, 138bl, 138tl, 138-139b, 139br, 139c, 139, 139tl, 140bl, 140cl, 140tr, 140-141c, 141, 142-143b, 142cl, 142tl, 142tr, 143t, 144bl, 144tr, 145tl, 146bl, 146tl, 146tr, 147tl, 150-151b, 151tr, 152bl, 152tr, 152-153c, 152tl, 153tr, 155, 159tl, 160c, 160tl, 160br, 163br, 164br, 180bl, 182tr, 182bl; Trackside Photo: 84tl, 84tr, 84-85bc, 85, 85t, 85br, 100bl, 100tr, 101, 101tr.

Jacket: Cover photograph: Allsports/Jim Lee. Back jacket photographs, clockwise from top left: Ron Lewis; Daytona Racing Archives; George Tiedemann; Daytona Racing Archives; Phil Cavali. Front Flap top: Daytona Racing Archives; bottom: George Tiedemann.